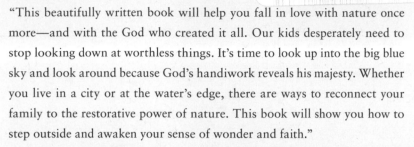

"This beautifully written book will help you fall in love with nature once more—and with the God who created it all. Our kids desperately need to stop looking down at worthless things. It's time to look up into the big blue sky and look around because God's handiwork reveals his majesty. Whether you live in a city or at the water's edge, there are ways to reconnect your family to the restorative power of nature. This book will show you how to step outside and awaken your sense of wonder and faith."

—Arlene Pellicane, host of the Happy Home podcast and author of
*Parents Rising* and *Screen Kids*

"We don't need more wonders in the world—just a greater sense of wonderment! With joy and practical know-how, Eryn Lynum helps parents connect the beauty of creation with love for the Creator. *Rooted in Wonder* is a must-read for helping the next generation to get outdoors and get to know God."

—Matthew Sleeth, MD, executive director of Blessed Earth and
author of *Reforesting Faith* and 24/6

"Do you want your children to be able to defend why they believe in God? *Rooted in Wonder* is the tool you need. Eryn Lynum masterfully connects Scripture to nature and nature to God. She includes ideas for fun activities and deeper conversations about creation and the Creator. This book will help you cultivate and strengthen your kids' faith and their ability to articulate why they believe what they believe. Well done!"

—Lori Wildenberg, national speaker, parent coach, and author of
*The Messy Life of Parenting*

"In an age of enslavement to digital devices and corrosive social media, Eryn Lynum brings parents—and indeed us all—a desperately needed message. If you want to see children grounded in what is real and true and good, get them *outside* with their hands in the dirt, their feet in puddles, and their eyes and ears and noses probing the wonders of God's creation. Lynum makes a compelling argument for not just sending the kids out to play, but also for joining them in their journey of discovery. In each chapter, practical tips are provided for things to try, and more importantly, how to help your kids see the connections between God's written word and his natural creations."

—Gregg Davidson, professor of geology & geological engineering at the University of Mississippi and author of *The Manifold Beauty of Genesis One*

"*Rooted in Wonder* is a soul-refreshing meditation that invites the reader to recover a sense of wonder and gratitude for God's magnificent artistry. With engaging prose and keen insights gleaned from both Scripture and nature, Lynum offers a trail map for the cultivation of a sacramental understanding of creation."

—Melissa Cain Travis, PhD, author of *Science and the Mind of the Maker*

"*Rooted in Wonder* perfectly ties together children's curiosity and God's faithfulness and creation. This book not only inspires but also gives practical ideas to embrace your child's natural wonder and teach kids about God through their experiences in nature. You will finish this book encouraged, equipped, adventurous, and ready to form a deeper connection with your kids and God as you delight in his creation."

—Steph Thurling, executive director of Christian Parenting and coauthor of *Raising Prayerful Kids*

"*Rooted in Wonder* makes its case well—opportunities abound to cultivate one's faith through the mystery and beauty of the natural world, and to develop an ethical relationship with it."

—Steve Swenson, the Aldo Leopold Foundation

"This book is a beautifully written, powerful treatment of the natural world as God's revelation to his people. The focus of Eryn Lynum's passionate writing is children and families and helping them get to know how studying nature can guide kids toward the majesty of God's creation. The author weaves theological insights with practical advice on how to instill a love for the natural word in kids of all ages. The sections of each chapter called 'Step Outside' are filled with activities and questions geared for a joyful educational experience. Lynum makes extensive use of biblical quotations, as well as her own experience as a mother of four and her qualifications as a certified naturalist, to provide a Christ-centered discovery and exploration of the created world of nature. This book will be a true blessing for you and your family."

—Sy Garte, PhD, author of *The Works of His Hands* and
editor-in-chief of *God and Nature*

"In an often chaotic and confusing world, God's creation not only provides a respite but also boldly and intricately reflects countless biblical principles that ground us. As parents, we have the privilege and responsibility to pass these timeless truths on to our children. In *Rooted in Wonder*, Eryn Lynum masterfully explains many biblical principles reflected in God's creation and by doing so she shows parents how to help their children make these connections as well. I encourage parents to read through this lovely book with an eye toward godly culture building by investing in their children who will then pass these lessons on to their children."

—Durenda Wilson, twenty-seven-year veteran homeschool mom of
eight, author of *The Unhurried Homeschooler* and *The Four-
Hour School Day*, and host of The Durenda Wilson Podcast

"*Rooted in Wonder* is a must-read with and for your family! Not only does Eryn help you understand the depths of God's love through nature, but she makes the outdoors a living classroom for you and your children. She will help open your eyes to both small and large miracles while experiencing God's creation and give you practical ways to help engage your children in the 'Step Outside' sections. If you're not much of an 'outdoorsy' type, you will be after reading this book. You will experience God's nature in new and curious ways, while putting into action Deuteronomy 6:7, 'You shall teach them diligently to your children when you sit in your house and when you walk by the way.' Prepare yourself for a collision with creation and curiosity as you encounter the wonder of God in a fresh and new way."

—Jessie Seneca, author, speaker, leadership trainer, and founder of More of Him Ministries

# ROOTED IN WONDER

# ROOTED
# IN
# WONDER

Nurturing Your Family's Faith
Through God's Creation

# ERYN
# LYNUM

KREGEL
PUBLICATIONS

Cataloging-in-Publication Data is available from the Library of Congress.

ISBN 978-0-8254-4761-7, print
ISBN 978-0-8254-7001-1, epub
ISBN 978-0-8254-7107-0, Kindle

Printed in the United States of America
24 25 26 27 28 29 30 31 32 / 5 4 3 2

*For Grayson. You have been wooing me to the
wilderness ever since you walked me into the
Vernon Marsh and asked me to marry you.*

*For Zeke, Ellis, Will, and Roary.
You reawaken my sense of wonder.*

# Contents

# Acknowledgments

I'M FOREVER GRATEFUL TO THOSE who made this book possible, whether by working directly on its publication or inspiring its message in my heart.

Creator God, you tucked curiosity into my soul then fanned its flame. Thank you for allowing me to share your wonders and truth. Thank you for creating a magnificently beautiful world.

Grayson, everything I do begins with you. You compel me forward. Any achievement was sparked by your encouragement. Thank you for convincing me I can do it, then coming with me each step of the way. You're my favorite adventure.

Zeke, Ellis, Will, and Roary, each of you shows me nature in a unique way. Your insightful perspectives and love for discovering new things inspire me every day. Thanks for adventuring with me.

Dad and Mom, you always showed me the Father's world. In our travels across the country and in equipping me to later travel the globe, you showed me there is always more to discover, learn, and share with others. Mom, your venture into becoming a master naturalist inspired me to embark on this journey. Dad, you've always pointed my attention and affections to the skies.

Scott and Chris, you raised an incredible man with adventure in his heart. Without him and the values you instilled in him, I could not have written this book.

Bob Hostetler, with the Steve Laube Agency, and the Kregel Publications team, you believed in this book from the start and made it happen.

Thank you.

# Fully Convinced

*For his invisible attributes, namely, his eternal power
and divine nature, have been clearly perceived, ever
since the creation of the world, in the things that have
been made. So they are without excuse.*

ROMANS 1:20

I CLOSED MY EYES, FILTERING the experience through only my listening ears, taking in the full range of the bull elk's bugle. His call echoed off the rocky cliffs, passing along one by one on countless blades of native grasses. His voice shivered between the early autumn aspen leaves before the river swallowed the sound. Another bull responded a mile away. Their eerie autumnal chorus rose across the valley.

Playing a few hundred yards from elk calves grazing with their mamas, our four children jumped between boulders behind my husband and me. The sun retreated below the horizon as we sipped soup and nibbled cornbread.

We come to this spot often. The entrance to Rocky Mountain National Park sits an hour's drive from our home down the mountain.

Yet this night was extra special and held a note of tradition. It was our fall soup picnic during the annual elk rut. We watched bulls charging one another, corralling cows and their young, and trotting triumphantly across the grasslands. A mama moose and her calf meandered into a pond, stopping for a drink beside dozens of elk—a scene right out of a safari magazine, only Rocky Mountain–style. I didn't say a word and offered no instruction or agenda for my children; I do not need to most of the time. Nature speaks for itself. At the metronome of God's pace, creation answers our questions, then teaches us to ask better ones.

At times, however, we need a framework for those questions and the discussions they introduce. Without understanding a good God who made everything and has a purpose for creation and our lives, we miss the depth of this conversation. Nature speaks for itself, but we need help translating its message. We need God's Word to make sense of his world. From this book I pray you will find the encouragement, knowledge, and resources to discern nature's messages and pass them along to your child. As you venture together into God's wild world, I pray you'll witness the incredible gift of your child's faith growing more resilient through the wonders of creation.

My family moved to the Rocky Mountains eight years ago. We didn't need to, but we saw the opportunity and took the 650-mile leap from where we were living in Kansas City. We yearned for a backdrop etched in wonder, one to preserve our children's intrigue with the natural world. I say we did not need to make this move because this type of education can be found wherever you are. Ours did not begin in the Rocky Mountains. Instead, it found its roots in the city. Its prelude was written into evening and weekend trips, wherever we could Tetris them into the margins of our weeks. In Kansas City, we sought out every pocket of forest we could find, visited the river almost daily, and memorized each step of the nature trails at the city's edge. We discovered that this access to the outdoor world is never far; we simply have to find it and make it our own. I imagine you share this desire. I'm guessing it's why you hold this book in your hands. You have felt, to some degree, the same pulse that grew exponentially in power through the veins of my family. My husband, Grayson, and I saw our children connecting with God in a profound way, and we knew we could not turn down such an opportunity. Instead, we needed to nurture it through as many outdoor hours as possible. Taking your child outside will become all the more powerful as you discover unique connections between God and creation. Nature will become the classroom in which you and your child discover, side by side, the nurturing and powerful love of our Creator.

In a society that says, "Your truth is true for you, and mine is true for me," we realize nature's potential to ground our children in reality. There are truths about God that we want our kids to understand but are unsure how to communicate. Nature provides new vocabulary. It also holds wonder. Glory shifts our gaze from what is temporal to what is eternal.

It did not take long for my children to surpass my knowledge of natural things. Curiosity propelled them far beyond my rusty capacity for attention and detail. In time, they began to teach me. They classed me in wonder as they arrived home from a morning of play at the river with a wagon full of fossils or a bucket of water bugs and an urgent need to identify them. As my son pointed to a bird atop a cottonwood branch and told me its name and what it likes to eat, I realized quickly this natural education takes on its own pace. We can provide rich resources and unmeasured hours outdoors, but it is our kids' curiosity that propels them. At times, I grew uncomfortable with the pace. I was desperate to keep up—to engage with my children in their interests and offer guardrails against misunderstandings. I wanted to give them a safe arena where their natural curiosities could develop into a wholesome view of the world. So

I enrolled in a course to become a master naturalist, compelled to synthesize this new field of study with my degree in biblical studies. How could I, in a world that often worships creation rather than the Creator, intelligently and graciously educate others about natural things and, in every detail, show how those facts and wonders point back to the One who so eloquently designed them? That question was the fertile soil for this book. In these pages I pray you will discover naturalism in its original and biblical sense. We can redeem it and dust off its secular decay. Naturalism is not the sterile, limited, void-of-anything-sacred study of nature—it is so much more! Nature provides us vivid imagery that we can tether to biblical truths so that our children readily remember them. Naturalism is an adventure in learning about creation so we can better understand and more deeply know our Creator.

Nature education is growing in style and popularity. Our generation has seen a sharp return to the soil and water, a pang of gnawing hunger for a simpler and more natural way of life. Yet I'm concerned at the cheap, shallow offerings I see. In many areas, the connection between creation and Creator has been severed. It is our responsibility and joy as parents or caregivers to reconnect the dots. We get to serve up a complete picture for our children. We can bring naturalism, the study of natural things, back to its rightful place as theology, an education of our Creator. We can offer our children an intellectual faith founded in tested scientific facts and nurtured through outdoor play. We can give them a resilient faith rooted in evidence and led with confidence.

Hebrews 11:1 says, "Now faith is the assurance of things hoped for, the conviction of things not seen." The root word for *assurance* means "substance," and the word for *conviction* alludes to "evidence." This level of faith is not wishful thinking—it is a confident, resilient, and unshakable faith. This is what our children's beliefs can be rooted in. Nature gives us the means, method, and materials to make it happen.

You do not need to move your family to the mountains to implement what is outlined in this book—although I'll warn you, it might cross your mind. Nor do you need to be a biologist or naturalist. My heart is to share simple and easy-to-implement ideas and activities that reconnect the dots between creation and Creator. As you reestablish this vital connection, your children will find themselves without excuse, fully convinced—or at the very least holding undeniable evidence—that there is a designer behind the universe's intricate details. Moreover, they will discover this designer delights in them even more than the flowers of the field or the birds of the air.

In these pages, you'll discover how God meets us and reveals himself through nature. At the close of each chapter, a "Step Outside" section will equip and inspire you to walk with your children into a deeper understanding of Scripture, nature, and what both teach us about God and his love for us. The Bible readings and activities will help develop your and your children's faith by synthesizing God's Word with his wonderful world. *Rooted in Wonder* is meant to introduce you to God's Word on a new and memorable level, and to equip you to teach your children who God is in engaging ways.

Deuteronomy has a well-worn passage instructing parents to diligently teach God's Word to their children. Deuteronomy 6:6–9 says:

> And these words that I command you today shall be on your heart. You shall teach them diligently to your children, and shall talk of them when you sit in your house, and when you walk by the way, and when you lie down, and when you rise. You shall bind them as a sign on your hand, and they shall be as frontlets between your eyes. You shall write them on the doorposts of your house and on your gates.

Although culture has shifted in countless ways since the writing of these words, the heart behind them remains steadfast. We are invited to dive deep into our faith, gain a deeper understanding of Scripture, and pass that knowledge and truth on to our children. "When you walk by the way" can look like a stroll along a riverside or a walk through the woods. "When you rise," you can sit outside with your children listening to the songs of the birds as a chorus of praise to our Creator. Occasionally, "when you lie down" might be beneath a canopy of stars declaring the glory of God.

What strikes me about these instructions in Deuteronomy is that the first command is not about our kids—it's about us: "These words that I command you today shall be on *your* heart" (emphasis added).

This work begins first in us.

Perhaps what surprised me most as I began stepping into nature with my family was not how it affected my kids, but how it impacted my own faith.

Wherever you are in your faith journey and whatever your understanding of Scripture and nature, God wants to meet you in these pages. Before we dive in and begin discovering God in nature, take time to sit outside and journal a prayer. Ask God to show you his Word in a new way through this book. Ask him to equip you to be a parent "rightly handling the word of truth," as we read in 2 Timothy 2:15. Ask him to grow your affection for his Word and draw your attention to how he uses nature narratives throughout Scripture. Ask him to teach you practical ways to incorporate his Word into your and your family's everyday adventures. Ask him to show you new opportunities to point your children to their Creator through his creation—that together you may become those eagerly searching out his signatures and likeness in this beautiful world.

Consider using the prayer below as a guide or writing your own:

Dear Lord,

I want to know you more. I recognize you have left your signatures throughout nature, and I want to spend my days seeking them out and learning new-to-me truths about who you are and how you care for my family. Train my attention on the details of creation. Show me every playful, colorful, fragrant, and intricate detail you've tucked into the outside world for me to find.

Finally, Lord, show me how to point my child's eyes to you in creation. Help me become familiar with how you use nature in your teachings and then take my children outside and share those lessons with them. Strip away any insecurity or feeling of inadequacy—I want to take this journey alongside my children and watch you work wonders in our faith. Help us to step outside and meet you amid all you have made. Amen.

Johannes Kepler, a renowned astronomer in the 1500s through 1600s, used his scientific understanding to point others to the evidence for God found throughout the universe. Kepler wrote,

> Thus God himself
> Was too kind to remain idle.
> And began to play the game of signatures,
> Signing his likeness into the world.[1]

If God intentionally left us hints as to who he is and who we are, may we faithfully seek out those clues. It begins by stepping outside in nature.

—Eryn Lynum
Wife to Grayson
Mama of four
Certified master naturalist sharing the truth of God's Word
through the wonders of his creation

# This Is My Father's World

*This is my Father's world:*
*I rest me in the thought*
*Of rocks and trees, of skies and seas—*
*His hand the wonders wrought.*
MALTBIE DAVENPORT BABCOCK

WHEN YOU THINK ABOUT NATURE, are your thoughts naturally drawn to God? Many of us make a subconscious connection between nature and God. Yet have you ever felt this connection as passive—a brief and incomplete historical outline in the Bible's introduction—and struggled to see how it affects daily life? As you practice seeing God in nature and becoming familiar with the nature narrative throughout Scripture, you'll become proficient in taking your children outside and pointing them to their Creator in fun and memorable ways. As you do, your children's faith will deepen. They will gain resilience, responsibility, an eye for beauty, and they will develop a healthier mindset. They will practice recognizing God all around them.

I watched this education taking shape in my family on a trip we took out West to see a bunch of bones. The landscape was desolate. Perhaps October was not an opportune time to venture to Utah, yet here we were—with a tired SUV packed with our four children and black Labrador. Dinosaur Monument National Park had long been on our radar, ever since our geologist neighbor told us about a vast land punctuated with fossils and geological wonders.

My sons' budding interests in geology and paleontology led us to book the trip. For four days, we explored the sprawling landscape of Dinosaur Monument. The park bridges Colorado and Utah. We explored the Utah side first, with walls of fossilized dinosaur bones. The main attraction is a petrified river dam of bones. An exhibit sign told us that the dinosaurs died from famine. The river swept their bodies along until they piled up where we stood now. A dam formed, fossilized, and was later discovered in the early 1900s.

The Colorado side of the park boasts fewer fossils but is nonetheless a wonder. We drove for hours through the endless, stretching space. Dirt road gave way to another dirt road. Finally, we wound down a precariously steep road until rock cliffs hemmed us in. It was midweek, and we had the entire canyon to ourselves. The Green River bends at nearly a 180-degree angle around Ship Rock, a magnificent sheer face of a mountain.

Most of the land, however, is not characterized by water. Most of it is desert, dry and dusty. The only life sustained are batches of sagebrush and juniper trees—the only foliage resilient enough for these parched lands. The anomaly is the river. Where it winds through the desert, a ribbon of tall cottonwood trees follows. Perhaps October was not a poor choice of timing after all, as the cottonwoods were glowing yellow. They added a splash of bright color to the valley.

"Mom," our oldest son called from the back seat, "I know now why the trees grow by the river. They need the water for their roots."

He voiced his thoughts as we drove across the sage-carpeted panorama. Slicing through the dry land was this procession of fifty-foot-tall cottonwoods, thick with leaves shivering gold in the breeze.

"You're right," I told him. "It's like in Psalm 1, when we read about a tree firmly planted by streams of water, whose leaf does not wither, and who produces fruit in each season."

This image is echoed by the prophet Jeremiah in Jeremiah 17:7–8.

> Blessed is the man who trusts in the LORD,
>      whose trust is the LORD.
> He is like a tree planted by water,
>      that sends out its roots by the stream,
> and does not fear when heat comes,
>      for its leaves remain green,
> and is not anxious in the year of drought,
>      for it does not cease to bear fruit.

The one who trusts in the Lord will not fear the heat and will produce fruit during a drought. I saw it now. The cottonwoods didn't look anxious.

Can you picture your children with a faith rooted in the living waters of God's Word? Our kids are growing up in an unpredictable and ever-changing world. Yet whatever drought seasons or circumstances they encounter, they can walk forward with confidence rather than anxiety. They can thrive in a desert.

Perhaps this was the observation made by Maltbie Davenport Babcock when he penned his poem, which later became the hymn "This Is My Father's World." The refrains were inspired by his regular walks up the hill by his home to gain a sweeping view of Lake Ontario. "I'm going out to see my Father's world,"[1] Babcock would tell his wife, Katherine, on the way out the door. Babcock knew the power of submerging himself in the wonders of creation. He knew the centering force of it all—the allure of rocks and trees, birds and seas, and how it jolts our worries away from the world and sets our thoughts on the power and beauty of our Maker.

My son saw it that day at Dinosaur Monument, how even in a desert, there is a stream of living water—a river promising life. Psalm 1:1–3 tells us:

> Blessed is the man
>> who walks not in the counsel of the wicked,
> nor stands in the way of sinners,
>> nor sits in the seat of scoffers;
> but his delight is in the law of the LORD,
>> and on his law he meditates day and night.

> He is like a tree
>> planted by streams of water
> that yields its fruit in its season,
>> and its leaf does not wither.
> In all that he does, he prospers.

You can practice meditating, or thinking deeply, on God's words and ways alongside your children as you explore how God reveals himself to us in his Word and in nature. God provides for us two creative revelations of who he is, and they work in harmony to bring us closer to himself.

## Two Ways God Reveals Himself to Us, and How They Work Together

God wants your children to know him deeply. Therefore, he has provided resources for you to understand who he is, how he loves us, and how to introduce these truths to your children. In a winding column of cottonwoods clinging to a river's edge outside Dinosaur, Colorado, my son gained an unforgettable image of what it looks like to meditate on God's Word day and night; to be like a firmly planted tree. This is the power of our Father's world: his landscapes lend powerful visuals for our children to perceive his love and might.

Theologians—those who study God and the Bible—refer to this concept as *natural revelation*. I first heard this term in Bible college. We learned about the two primary ways God reveals himself to us:

- *Special revelation*, referring to what we learn about God through his written Word, the Scriptures.
- *Natural revelation*, encompassing all we learn about God through what he has made, as outlined in Romans 1:20, "For his invisible attributes, namely, his eternal power and divine nature, have been clearly perceived, ever since the creation of the world, in the things that have been made. So they are without excuse."

Nearly two decades would pass from the time I learned the difference before I began to grasp how these two revelations complement one another. My son said it so well that day in the valley. A string of cottonwoods dressing the river acted as a perfect example of natural revelation highlighting special revelation—a painted picture of Psalm 1 and Jeremiah 17. In the tangible trees, waterways, and creatures of the earth, we can comprehend the intangible concepts of abiding, growing, fellowshipping, and thriving.

Have you ever found yourself in a season of life that felt like a drought? Maybe you've experienced a lack or loss of community, or a time in which your faith felt stunted and impossible to grow. Have you watched your children struggling with questions or doubts in their faith? God provides visuals in nature to help us glimpse the beauty and strength he can bring during those difficult times.

Let me be clear: I believe the Bible in itself is sufficient. If I spent my life locked up in a room without windows yet had the Word of

God, I'd be dreadfully sad in missing the outdoors, but I would not be without hope. God's Word is sufficient to communicate his great love and salvation to us. We see this in Isaiah 55:11: "My word . . . that goes out from my mouth; it shall not return to me empty, but it shall accomplish that which I purpose, and shall succeed in the thing for which I sent it." By reading verse 10 and keeping this passage in context, however, we find the nature connection:

> For as the rain and the snow come down from heaven
>     and do not return there but water the earth,
> making it bring forth and sprout,
>     giving seed to the sower and bread to the eater,
> so shall my word be that goes out from my mouth;
>     it shall not return to me empty,
> but it shall accomplish that which I purpose,
>     and shall succeed in the thing for which I sent it.

Rain and snow lend depth, a poignant and memorable visual of God's Word bringing forth fruit and life.

There is a word that carries the specific scent of this visual. *Petrichor* is the wet, earthy aroma aroused by spring rain. Close your eyes and think back to an experience where you have stepped outside after a spring rain. Can you remember the scent? One whiff of it offers a fragrant promise: the earth is ready to grow good things. You can pray for this petrichor effect in your children's soul, that their spirits are wet and waiting for the seed of God's truth and promises.

Nature is a secondary revelation; it cannot stand alone. In *Leave Only Footprints*, author Conor Knighton shares his spiritual journey alongside others who have sought and discovered God in the wilderness. Left and right, he quotes John Muir, the famed naturalist who was also a firm believer.

As I read, I connected with Knighton's points. As he summed up the chapter, however, I found an eloquently written yet disheartening conclusion, which also proves nature as an incomplete revelation of God. Knighton wrote, "I want to feel connected to something greater than myself, and I do feel that. But I no longer think there's one specific path that leads to enlightenment or salvation."[2]

Nature had showed him God, but not his need for Jesus.

Romans 1:20 tells us that God's attributes are apparent in nature, so humankind is without excuse as to his existence. Nature, however, has a more challenging time communicating the gospel, or the good news that Jesus came to rescue us. James 2:19 says, "You believe that God is one; you do well. Even the demons believe—and shudder!"

Satan also knows God exists. He sees God's hand throughout nature and shudders. Then he sets himself to work destroying all God has made.

Nature shows us a creative, sovereign, and powerful God. It's harder to hear from the birds' songs or perceive from the mountains that Jesus died to save us from our sins and rose to give us new life. Once we know him, we see it everywhere: he is the bringer of new life. But we need God's living, active, and convicting Word to show us our need for him. Romans 3:23–24 says, "For all have sinned and fall short of the glory of God, and are justified by his grace as a gift, through the redemption that is in Christ Jesus."

God's Word plainly states the gospel message and tells us how we can be saved from our sins. Romans 10:9 says, "If you confess with your mouth that Jesus is Lord and believe in your heart that God raised him from the dead, you will be saved."

Have you wondered how to present the gospel message to your children? It can feel like a hefty task. Yet in his Word, God has given us clear instructions: admit and turn away from our sins, and accept and follow him as our Lord and Savior. Further, in creation he's given us visuals to help our children better understand God's character and compassion. If your children are too young to grasp the gospel message, you can prepare them now through prayer. Ask God to help your little ones see and sense his presence outdoors, so they will better understand his message and love when they're ready to make a choice to follow him.

Nature might lead us to thoughts of God, which can spark curiosity that will guide us to his Word, but nature by itself is not a complete dictionary. Instead, it is an interpretive tool for our primary revelation: God's Word. It is a commentary, offering a broader understanding of what the Scriptures say. C. S. Lewis said it this way: "Nature never taught me that there exists a God of glory and of infinite majesty. I had to learn that in other ways. But nature gave the word *glory* a meaning for me. I still do not know where else I could have found one."[3]

Nature guides us in understanding, visualizing, and internalizing who God is and what that means for us. We discover his character and creativity, and how he interacts with humanity. This biblical study of natural things is centuries old. Observations of nature began in the garden of Eden. But throughout written history, we see traces of these narratives; inklings of wonderings penned from those taking a significant step beyond simple nature philosophy or natural history and into natural theology. Those who study natural theology show us a progression from nature, to creation, to Creator. Many well-known nature theologians—drawing concrete observations about who God is from what he has made—wrote of nature as a "book" by which we absorb profound truths concerning our Creator. As we immerse our children in the chapters of such a book, they memorize the narrative. They fall in love with the language. They intimately meet their Maker.

But what do we do when our children ask questions about nature that we don't have answers to? Is there opportunity in the unknowns to uphold the creation-Creator connection? At times my children ask questions that stretch beyond my knowledge of nature. I don't understand how some things work. The greatest scientists to ever live also struggled with this tension. Yet I find that God does not owe us an explanation for how or why he created. Instead, he left details yet to be discovered and tucked curiosity into the heart of humanity. He hinted at wonder, then let us loose. In her book *Science and the Mind of the Maker*, author Melissa Cain Travis explains this concept as the "Maker Thesis." Part one of the Maker Thesis is this: our universe was fine-tuned and created both intellectually and strategically for life to exist. Part two adds: God created humans with a unique intellectual capacity to discover the secrets of what he has made. Travis writes, "Because God's intellect is reflected, to a finite extent, in his image-bearers, we are naturally inclined to detect signs of the Maker in his workmanship."[4] And a few chapters later, she summarizes, "It is as if we were *meant* to uncover the secrets of the world around us."[5]

Before humankind had the entirety of the Scriptures, they had nature, and we find them time and again using it to discover God, as in Job 12:7–10:

> But ask the beasts, and they will teach you;
>     the birds of the heavens, and they will tell you;
> or the bushes of the earth, and they will teach you;
>     and the fish of the sea will declare to you.
> Who among all these does not know
>     that the hand of the LORD has done this?
> In his hand is the life of every living thing
>     and the breath of all mankind.

Beasts of the field, birds of the air, plants of the ground, and fish of the sea have something to say about God. We can help our children attune their ears to listen.

## "In the Beginning" Was Just the Beginning

In Genesis, we find a summary of God's acts of creation. It serves as a prelude to the nature narrative that God builds upon throughout Scripture. In books like Job and Psalms, we're afforded a broader perspective of what happened as God spoke the world into place. As you become familiar with these passages that expound on creation, you will discover that God never intended nature to be a one-and-done thing. Your mind will create connections between what he did back at creation and what it means for your life and faith.

You see, God is a storyteller. He is an author. There is a doctrine in Christianity that explains this concept. It is called progressive revelation and supposes that God gradually built a story through the Bible. Early on, he hinted at truths that he elaborated on later in the Bible. Have you ever experienced something in your life that made little or no sense to you at the time? Perhaps with time's passing you can see reasons the event took place, or at least what you learned or how you grew through that experience. God progressively reveals his plans in his perfect timing. Progressive revelation proposes the idea that God withheld some details because humanity couldn't quite handle them yet. Perhaps as he reveals more of his plans over time, they make a bigger impact, or we grow more through the process of trusting him in unknowns. Here are three examples of where God hinted at how he made the universe, then later gave more detail.

### God Commands Light

In Genesis 1:3–5 (NASB), we read how God spoke light into existence: "God said, 'Let there be light'; and there was light. God saw that the light was good; and God separated the light from the darkness. God called the light 'day,' and the darkness He called 'night.' And there was evening and there was morning, one day."

In Job 38:12–13 (NASB), we're given a more vivid picture: "Have you ever in your life commanded the morning, and made the dawn know its place, so that it would take hold of the ends of the earth?"

### God Commands the Water

In Genesis 1:9–10 (NASB), we find God dividing the waters into an organized system: "God said, 'Let the waters below the heavens be gathered into one place, and let the dry land appear'; and it was so. And God called the dry land 'earth,' and the gathering of the waters He called 'seas'; and God saw that it was good."

Psalm 104:5–10 offers us a poetic explanation:

> He set the earth on its foundations,
>     so that it should never be moved.
> You covered it with the deep as with a garment;
>     the waters stood above the mountains.
> At your rebuke they fled;
>     at the sound of your thunder they took to flight.
> The mountains rose, the valleys sank down
>     to the place that you appointed for them.
> You set a boundary that they may not pass,
>     so that they might not again cover the earth.
>
> You make springs gush forth in the valleys;
>     they flow between the hills.

### God Commands the Heavens

In Genesis 1:14–17 we find God stringing together the night sky on the fourth day of creation. "And God said, 'Let there be lights in the expanse of the heavens to separate the day from the night. And let them be for signs and for seasons, and for days and years, and let them be lights in the expanse of the heavens to give light upon the earth.'

And it was so. And God made the two great lights—the greater light to rule the day and the lesser light to rule the night—and the stars. And God set them in the expanse of the heavens to give light on the earth."

God's words to Job 38:31–33 (NASB) expound:

> Can you tie up the chains of the Pleiades,
> Or untie the cords of Orion?
> Can you bring out a constellation in its season,
> And guide the Bear with her satellites?
> Do you know the ordinances of the heavens,
> Or do you establish their rule over the earth?

History tells an elaborate story of experts who have studied the night sky and what lies beyond our atmosphere. Author Matthew Sleeth shares the truly spectacular essence of this passage in Job, written long before our historians, mathematicians, philosophers, and astronomers would make such discoveries. Sleeth writes:

> It almost seems as if God were daring us to invent the telescope and have a look-see for ourselves. In all these questions God was suggesting an order, timing, and laws that neither Job nor humanity were yet aware of, much less understood. We read these statements and others like them in the Bible through a fog of repetition and familiarity. As a result, we miss the wonders of God's questions. How could any author other than the Creator of the universe know to ask them?[6]

There was no basis, no context, and no dictionary to explain what God was suggesting in Job 38. There were yet to be instruments by which it could be measured, experimented on, or tested. Thus, only the One who had set it all into motion back in Genesis could offer such detailed expression. We live in our Father's world, and it seems as though he is still using progressive revelation. As science, tools, and technology develop, we discover more about who he is. The truth has always been there. Our job is to keep searching for his likeness in nature.

For far too long, I stopped at the creation story. I let my unanswered questions grow stale. I grew complacent with the simplicity of Genesis. As a child in Sunday school, I memorized the days of creation and what God made on each day. I didn't know to ask further questions or consider other passages that might add more to the story. In Bible college, as I grew more familiar with Bible study methods, I learned to consider Scripture passages in their immediate context (what verses came before and after them) and in the context of the Bible as a whole. I learned I could play connect-the-dots across God's Word, gaining a fuller picture of his intent.

Finally, as I began spending more time out in creation, I learned to ask questions of Scripture: Why did God create the waterway systems like he did? What can a solar or lunar eclipse tell us about his detailed timing? How can perennial flowers, whose roots persevere through winter and bloom again each spring, relate to what God says about resilience and new life after hardship?

I began noticing the rich and robust nature narratives threading Scripture together. I realized God was only setting the stage in Genesis, and he further expounded on the glory of his works throughout the following sixty-five books of the Bible. In this way, God models an incredibly effective method for teaching our children.

Above I gave only three examples from creation: God commanding light, water, and the heavens. We have yet even to hit on vegetation, creatures of the oceans and skies, animals roaming the earth, and of course, our existence as relational human beings created in God's image. All of these magnificent and miraculous creations are offered a handful of verses here at the outset of Earth's history. But Genesis

was only the prelude, and God was not finished with the poetic litera-
ture of nature. He would continue to draw from what he had created
to communicate who he is and how he loves us.

In Hebrews 4:12, we read, "For the word of God is living and
active." We believe this concerning the special revelation of everything written in the Bible. We can also experience it from his natural
revelation. You can hear it in a bird's morning song. You can see it
in the silhouette of willow leaves draping over a river or tall grass
swaying in a breeze. You can smell it from wildflowers. God's creation is breathing, singing, and praising. It is living and active, all of
it proclaiming who he is. The verse continues to explain that God's
Word is "sharper than any two-edged sword, piercing to the division
of soul and of spirit, of joints and of marrow, and discerning the
thoughts and intentions of the heart." Maybe you've experienced this
life-altering power of Scripture with a Bible open on your lap. You
can know it also in the unmatched stillness of a hushed forest, surrounded by aspen and ponderosa pine, or in the breeze of a salty sea.

Nothing has ever discerned the thoughts and intentions of my
heart like his Word . . . or his woods.

## Step Outside

The most effective way you can introduce your children to God
through nature is by becoming familiar with his Word and his created world. His *special revelation* (the Bible) and *natural revelation*
(creation) are his gifts to us, and the primary resources we have for
teaching our kids about God's qualities and activities.

Don't become overwhelmed by all there is to know, and don't buy
into the enemy's lie that you're not qualified. God has called you to
this wonderful task, and he is equipping you for it. You can begin simply by exploring the creation story in Genesis. The days of creation
are building blocks on which your children will construct a resilient

faith rooted in the wonder of creation. As your children spend more time exploring God's Word and nature, they will recognize that this is our Father's world, and they have a place and purpose in it.

### See Nature in the Bible

As you begin opening God's Word with your children and exploring how God uses nature in Scripture, do so imaginatively! Start with the foundation of creation in Genesis 1. Consider using an easier-to-understand Bible translation such as the New International Version, New Century Version, or New Living Translation. Read Genesis 1:1–8 and talk about how God was setting the stage for life. By creating light and putting water droplets in the air, he was preparing Earth to be home for everything alive. Then as you explore together the days of creation, ask your children what their favorite thing is that God created on each day.

- Read Genesis 1:9–10. Would your children rather play at the ocean, in a creek or pond, or on a river or lake? What's their favorite thing to do in the water?
- Read Genesis 1:11–13. What is their favorite plant? Do they like climbing trees or picking flowers? What is their favorite fruit to eat that comes from a plant?
- Read Genesis 1:14–19. Do your children most enjoy watching a sunrise, sunset, or lying beneath a starry night sky? Have they ever seen a shooting star?
- Read Genesis 1:20–23. What are your children's favorite birds? What are their favorite sea creatures? Can they imagine a world without birds, or without any fish, whales, or dolphins?
- Read Genesis 1:24–25. What are your children's favorite animals that walk on land? What might Earth be like without those animals? Do those animals have important jobs?
- Read Genesis 1:26–27. Who are some people your children are

so glad God created? It might be family members, close friends, or people from history. Talk about how God has important plans and purposes for all people, including your children. Share with your children that you are so grateful God created them.

### See God in Nature

Take your children outside and ask them to choose something natural they see. It can be insects, flowers or other plants, bodies of water, mammals, birds—anything God has made. Then ask the following questions:

- What do you think God was thinking about when he created this?
- What strengths did he give it?
- What details about God does it reflect?

If they have difficulty with this, help them choose another object and try again. Consider themes like strength, resilience, joy, energy, beauty, provision, wonder, playfulness, creativity, and wisdom.

# Reconnecting the Dots Between Creation and Creator

*God communicates to us through each other and through organized religion, through wise people and the great books, through music and art, [but nowhere] with such texture and forcefulness in detail and grace and joy, as through creation.*

ROBERT F. KENNEDY JR.

HAVE YOUR CHILDREN EVER DOUBTED their faith? As they grow older, their friends will ask questions or say things that will cause your children to falter in their beliefs. These threats can become opportunities. You don't have to be nervous about oppositions to your and your children's faith. You don't have to feel vulnerable or unqualified if your children ask questions you don't have answers for. That is the beautiful thing about nurturing your family's faith: you and your children get to take this journey side by side! You don't have to have all the answers. Instead, as you learn to ask the right questions about nature and the Bible, you can guide your children to a resilient faith that withstands society's faulty arguments.

Many of the false ideas your children will encounter come from humanity's desperation to find answers to their questions about life. We can prepare our kids by showing them where to look for answers. Many of us go through life searching for big signs. We want an answer to our questions, yet we refuse to quiet ourselves and train our attention. We want explanations for this world and our lives, for the human experience and purpose. If we're not careful, we're apt to grasp for shiny answers or whatever is served up in our school systems and media. All the while, so many explanations exist in our periphery, waiting and wanting to be discovered.

Each spring, we're afforded a brilliant miracle around our feet. Tiny Draba flowers carpet vast expanses of earth, whispering promises of a new growing season ready to unfold. Yet we often miss the delicate Draba while watching for the bright flowering trees or majestic tulips. Aldo Leopold wrote in *A Sand County Almanac*, "He who hopes for spring with upturned eye never sees so small a thing as Draba. . . . He who searches for spring with his knees in the mud finds it, in abundance."[1]

This is, I fear, how we often seek to answer the question of whether a Creator or a coincidence led to our existence. We are looking for big answers, ignoring the subtle hints all around us. Only when we press knees into the mud and examine the often-overlooked details will we see it—miracle and method, purpose and passion, intelligence and ingenuity—all at our feet, before our eyes, echoing through our ears, whetting our taste buds, and restoring our spirits. The late educator Charlotte Mason once wrote, "The child has truly a great deal to do before he is in a condition to 'believe his own eyes'; but Nature teaches so gently, so gradually, so persistently, that he is never overdone, but goes on gathering little stores of knowledge about whatever comes before him."[2]

When Galileo introduced the telescope as a tool to peer into the galaxies, his contemporaries did not believe him. Scoffing, they refused to even look through the device. Galileo sat alone with his telescope. He was the sole observer of the vastness of the cosmos. A single witness of galaxies beyond anything anyone had seen or imagined. Galileo had the stars to himself.

Undermining Aristotle's previous explanations of the universe, Galileo published his own findings based on what he'd seen through the telescope. He painted a picture for the entire world through words, a display of the heavens scratched across bound pages. He wrote about mountains and craters on the moon, spots upon the sun, satellites orbiting Jupiter, and multitudes of stars never known to exist. They were monumental discoveries that would shape future space explorations, but they fell on ears refusing to hear and eyes refusing to see. Galileo's peers mocked him and his toy. Strictly adhering to Aristotle's descriptions of the universe, they refused to believe anything contrary to what they had held to for so long.

Desperate for the world to glimpse what he'd seen—to understand how boundless the cosmos is—Galileo turned to astronomer Johannes Kepler for help. Kepler was a devoted follower of Christ who used math, science, and the pursuit of the stars to point others to the Creator. Kepler stood beside Galileo when no one else would. We overhear Galileo's frustrations in a letter addressed to Kepler in August 1610. The letter is preserved in Antonio Favaro's *Le Opere di Galileo Galilei* (*The Works of Galileo Galilei*), published in Italy across twenty volumes from the late 1800s through the early 1900s.[3] The following is a widely accepted translation:

My dear Kepler, I wish that we might laugh at the remarkable stupidity of the common herd. What do you have to say about the principal philosophers of this academy who are filled with the stubbornness of an asp and do not want to

look at either the planets, the moon or the telescope, even
though I have freely and deliberately offered them the opportunity a thousand times? Truly, just as the asp stops its ears,
so do these philosophers shut their eyes to the light of truth.[4]

How do you see today's society shutting their eyes to the light of
truth? They want your children to close their eyes also. You can be
the one who keeps your children's eyes open to truth and wonder.

Referring to a cultural tradition, Galileo called on the imagery
of an asp (viper) stopping its ears to the enchantment of a snake
charmer, turning one ear to the ground while twisting its tail up and
over the other ear. Did Galileo's contemporaries think him nothing
more than a snake charmer uttering absurdities to turn them away
from their long-held yet evidence-weak beliefs? Did they think he
was tickling their ears with superstition?

Compelled by his convictions to further the discoveries of what
God has made, Kepler stood beside Galileo and convinced the world
to look through the telescope. In a response letter to Galileo, Kepler's
words beamed with optimism and faith in future discoveries and
resulting applications. He wrote, "There will certainly be no lack
of human pioneers when we have mastered the art of flight. In the
meantime, we shall prepare for the brave sky-travelers maps of the
celestial bodies."[5]

Galileo and Kepler would never hear Neil Armstrong declare
"The Eagle has landed" from the moon. They would never glimpse
the fruits of their tireless observations and calculations. Their publications would pave the way for space travel but never take themselves
beyond the earth's atmosphere. They—especially Kepler—worked in
faith. Do you sometimes feel the same? Raising children to love and
follow God is a long-game approach. While some of the fruit we will
never see, we can trust that God uses every ounce of our efforts. His
Word goes forth and does not return void. Don't be overwhelmed by

the big picture. Instead, ask yourself what you can do today—right now—to introduce your children to their Maker. Every time we read our children Scripture or take them outside and point them to their Creator matters. God sees your labors, and he will not let them go to waste.

Galileo's and Kepler's endeavors are a nod to Hebrews 11, where we read about the patriarchs of faith working toward rewards they would never themselves receive this side of heaven. We read of these heroes, "These all died in faith, not having received the things promised, but having seen them and greeted them from afar" (v. 13).

One of these heroes of faith, Abram (later renamed Abraham), could have used Galileo's invention. Over three thousand years before Galileo and Kepler's conversations, Abram stood beneath the night sky amidst a grove of oaks rooted in the dirt of Hebron. Abram lived in what we today call a "blackout zone," where artificial lights hold no power over celestial illumination. Today these areas are rare. The Bortle scale measures the visibility of our night sky by nine levels. In Abram's day, there was no need for such measurements. No light pollution vied for the skies. There were only perfect starry nights.

Have you ever stood beneath a sky cloaked in black, pierced so precisely by the stars that you can actually see them twinkling? On a few occasions, the image, like photographic paper, has seared itself into my memory. Like the film strip's negative, it causes a contrasting effect: the breathtaking experience of a star-struck blackened night casts light on our souls.

Long before Thomas Edison's light bulb would scale to the cities and lay claim to the night sky, Abram stared into the expanse, conversing with its Creator. Yet what he saw was limited by the naked eye. The night God made his covenant promise with Abram, the undisturbed sky would have revealed an expanse of endless stars. A perfect visual for God's promise. God took Abram outside. In

Genesis 15:5 God told Abram, "'Look toward heaven, and number the stars, if you are able to number them.' Then he said to him, 'So shall your offspring be.'"

This was enough for Abram. Verse 6 tells us, "And he believed the LORD, and he counted it to him as righteousness." It was saving faith.

Yet we have to wonder, what would Abram have thought if he had possessed Galileo's instrument that night? Can you imagine if Abram held in his hands an invention of God-glory-reflecting, man-made ingenuity from over three thousand years in the future? Peering through Galileo's telescope, Abram would have glimpsed exponentially more stars. He would have realized the even fuller extent of God's promise.

Had Kepler never convinced the world to look through Galileo's telescope, would we have ever set foot on the moon? Would we be sending rovers to Mars? Would we have demolished fanciful and frightful superstitions and arrived on sound evidence about how weather, revolutions, eclipses, and the aurora borealis work? Would we have seen the hands of a Maker behind these intricate, stunning designs?

Philosophers in Galileo's time "shut their eyes to the light of truth."[6] In so many ways, the world is still doing the same today. Creation is our telescope, through which we come to see and realize the depth and breadth of who God is and how he loves us. The otherwise unnoticed details of God's character and compassion are brought into focus through the lens of creation. Paul David Tripp calls this the "gloryscope." He writes, "The glories of the physical world don't reflect God's glory by happenchance. No, God specifically and carefully designed the physical world to reflect him, that is, to be the gloryscope that our poorly seeing eyes so desperately need. As the technician grinds the lens of a telescope for the best clarity and magnification possible, so God fashioned his world in such a way that it would bring his glory into view."[7] You can use this gloryscope to instill within your child a robust and resilient faith rooted in evidence and beauty.

The first telescope did not bear Galileo's fingerprints. This two-lens magnifying machine had quietly been circulating for some time. Yet no one had bothered to recognize its true potential; not until Galileo pointed it up. Everything changes when we look up. Nature becomes creation, magnifying every detailed hint of our Creator. King David wrote in Psalm 19:1, "The heavens declare the glory of God, and the sky above proclaims his handiwork." That is if we do not shut our eyes to the light of truth. Looking around, I see in today's society two main ways humanity stops up its ears and refuses to look through the revealing, magnifying telescope of creation. First, our world seeks to explain away intelligence. Second, we are prone to worship creation rather than Creator.

## Society Attempts to Explain Away Intelligence

Face flushed red and ankles ringed in dirt, my son sat at the kitchen table recounting conversations from an afternoon playing in the creek with neighborhood buddies. "He said he doesn't believe in God."

Hearing the careful articulation of thoughts in my son's tone, I'm always prompted to stop and listen; his body language tells me, *this is important.* "That's really interesting," I responded, carefully arranging my words. "He thinks that God and science can't go together. When really, we know they absolutely work together!"

We had recently finished reading *Case for a Creator for Kids* by Lee Strobel. Amidst the pages, we'd walked through hypothetical discussions and scenarios, examining evidence for a Creator discovered through science. Closing the book after we read the last page, my son walked away equipped to enter the "God and science" conversation.

Although he was reading novels on his own, I chose to walk beside my son through this book to open conversations and practice the defense of our faith. Now he was encountering real-life scenarios; an arena in which to practice 1 Peter 3:15, "Always being prepared to make a defense to anyone who asks you for a reason for the hope that is in you; yet do it with gentleness and respect."

Your children will encounter many opposing beliefs as they grow older. They'll find that those around them don't believe in a Creator. They'll listen to convincing arguments for how this world formed apart from intelligence or reason. They'll doubt what you have taught them. As we examine the evidence for our faith found throughout history and science, however, my prayer for your children and mine is that those doubts will be shallow; that they'll stand no chance against the deep reservoirs of knowledge and proof they have experienced in God's Word and his world.

### A Pilgrimage from Facts to Faith

Throughout history, many people have developed a resilient faith because they began at a point of doubt. Have you ever encountered someone with a deep level of spiritual stamina? It is a tenacious faith led with confidence. I have observed it most in those who pilgrimaged to faith via the waters of unbelief, including authors Lee Strobel and C. S. Lewis.

Lee Strobel used to be an atheist. After his wife, Leslie, began following Jesus, he set out to rescue her from what he perceived as a cult. He determined to prove Christianity false. He dove into research using his training and experience in law and as a journalist for the *Chicago Tribune*. He called on archaeologists, biologists, historians, theologians, and lawyers to gather a well-rounded view. His findings were not what he expected, and they led them straight to a confident and thoroughly convinced faith in God as Creator and Jesus as Savior. Lee shared:

> You know, it's just like God in His love and grace to meet people where they're at. Leslie didn't need a lot of historical

data and scientific evidence to come to faith. It's just not in her personality and nature, and she had a personal experience with God, and that's great. But I think God knew that you know, given my scepticism and my background in journalism and law, that it was gonna take evidence for me, and sure enough, He took me on a path to discover exactly what I needed to hear.[8]

C. S. Lewis, renowned author of the Chronicles of Narnia series, is another with a story of resilient faith formed through intellectual struggle. At age seventeen, Lewis shared with a childhood friend, "I believe in no religion. There is absolutely no proof for any of them, and from a philosophical standpoint Christianity is not even the best."[9] It would take him fifteen years to reverse that opinion.

The *Christian Broadcasting Network* shares about Lewis, "His conversion to a robust Christianity required years of intellectual struggle and came only after being convinced that faith was reasonable."[10]

I wonder if Lewis's copious amounts of time outdoors influenced his intellectual arrival at Christianity. *Publishers Weekly* shares that as an adolescent, "He loved to take ten, fifteen, and twenty mile rapid tromps across countryside, but especially over rugged hills and mountains. He loved to ride a bicycle all over Oxfordshire. He loved to swim in cold streams and ponds. He loved to row a boat."[11] Could it be that as his feet put miles behind him, surrounded by natural beauty and the complexities of creation, Lewis learned to ask the questions that would lead him straight to God?

These apologists, or people building sound arguments and convincing claims based on evidence, exhibit incredible faith; not because they have stretched their belief muscles to squirm around unanswerable questions, but because they have dug deep into archives and evidence. Their faith is rooted in fact. I imagine it is the same agile faith you desire for your children—a faith powerful in both offense and defense. We can raise our children to have a quick and responsive faith, and yet, in the words of 1 Peter 3:15, characterized by "gentleness and respect." This is another quality I see in the faith of the apologists. They are empathetic and understanding toward those who are still shutting a blind eye or stopping up their ears to the truth. They understand what it's like to be in darkness. In a society loud and abrasive with opinions, you can train your children to stand firm in their beliefs and uphold the truth while showing love and respect.

David C. Downing, author of several award-winning books about C. S. Lewis, shares, "As Lewis himself said, he certainly remembered 'what Christianity looks like from the outside.' He understood atheism, he felt the force of its arguments in his bones and sinews. . . . Lewis's enduring influence as a Christian thinker is assuredly due in no small part to the fact that he spent so many years as a non-Christian thinker."[12]

Familiarity with the hole-filled alternatives lends confidence to our faith. Sharing with our kids stories of those who have arrived at faith through evidence is powerful. You can find our recommended reads at www.erynlynum.com/bookshelf. From these narratives, our kids can picture the pilgrimages these people have taken: the questions they asked, doubts they grappled with, and how they arrived at their conclusions. Our faith and that of our kids, however, cannot rest in others' stories. Our kids need their own experiences. They need to draw their own conclusions. Gleaning wisdom from those who have gone before them, they can weigh their questions against God's Word, emphasized by time in creation, and with these resources and experiences, God's Spirit can guide them to an unshakable faith.

### Science Points to a Creator
Science has long sought to explain away the rhyme and reason we see in nature. And yet, science has, whether intentionally or not, at the

same time proven the purpose we see in Earth's operations. Author Melissa Cain Travis proposes this in *Science and the Mind of the Maker·* "What if there are signs of intelligence in nature that can be detected through scientific investigation? If we rule out this possibility from the start, we are artificially limiting what nature is permitted to tell us."[13] Science untainted by bias and rightly conducted reveals evidence of intelligence and ingenuity.

My father is skilled in this scientific investigation. He was the teacher every child in our church wanted for their Sunday school class when I was growing up. He knew how to grab and keep a child's attention: through explosions. My dad was known to carry beakers and chemicals into the church to prove God through science while (thankfully, successfully) not burning down the church gymnasium. It wasn't only between the church walls that I received this education. My parents would regularly wake my brother, sister, and me in the middle of the night to witness a lightning storm. On other occasions, they drove us far beyond the reach of the town's streetlights to climb up on the roof of our car and watch a meteorite shower or the ribboning lights of aurora borealis dancing across the sky. Every experience was another page in my documentation of evidence. God is real. I was fully convinced back then, and even more so now as I pour into my kids' collections of experiences with their Creator.

You can present the same fun and wonder-filled education to your children. Spending time in creation, they will naturally ask questions that together you can seek out answers to. This is an organic way of building a worldview. Guided by God's Word and Spirit, your children (and you!) will experience a new depth of faith that snuffs out false ideas built on faulty foundations, such as evolution.

The discussion of creation versus coincidence increased in volume in the age of Darwinism. To some extent, this conversation has lent depth to Christianity. It forces us to abandon mere assumptions of the creation narrative. Instead, we must dissect it, challenging and questioning it as the world does. Then we can ultimately decide, with evidence in hand, whether or not we'll stake our life on the concept of a Creator. This is valuable for your children. As they watch you asking hard questions and digging into your faith, they'll understand it's ok to not have all the answers. They will observe the worthwhile endeavor of asking hard questions, thinking critically, and coming to their own conclusions.

While many are familiar with Charles Darwin's contributions to scientific history and the evolution theory, I was surprised by some lesser-known tidbits of his story. Darwin was a torn man. He was a divided soul if ever he believed in such a thing. After writing *On the Origin of Species* and *The Descent of Man* and birthing the theory of evolution, Darwin wrote in his own autobiography:

> Another source of conviction in the existence of God, con-nected with the reason and not with the feelings, impresses me as having much more weight. This follows from the extreme difficulty or rather impossibility of conceiving this immense and wonderful universe, including man with his capacity of looking far backwards and far into futurity, as the result of blind chance or necessity. When thus reflecting I feel compelled to look to a First Cause having an intelligent mind in some degree analogous to that of man; *and I deserve to be called a Theist.*[14]

After all his philosophizing, he could not escape the evidence of an intelligent mind behind what he saw in nature. Let us not only look at one side of the story but also carefully and prayerfully dissect the opposing sides. May we not hold to our creation narrative without knowing the other arguments and what real evidence there is for our faith. Although I disagree with Darwin on many levels, may we, like him, upon reflecting feel compelled to look to a "First Cause." And for goodness' sake, may our children, in the midst of being taught Darwinism as fact instead of theory, know this part of the story. Not even Darwin was fully convinced of his suppositions

If Darwin could not deny hints of an intelligent mind in drawing close to nature, then what might we glean from nature as we at the same time draw context from the Creator's words?

## Society Worships Creation Rather than Creator

"A lizard!" My son's voice ricocheted off scattered boulders, slicing through the chatter amongst visitors snapping photos.

"Mom, a lizard!"

His older and younger brothers followed the exclamation like bugs to a spotlight. The small reptile scurried into a crevice inside a boulder. The boys peered into the dark abysses of rock universe. Scooping up their baby sister, I secured her to the carrier on my back and maneuvered down a boulder to join the boys.

There was a field of them—these massive rocks—appearing more as if they sprouted from the ground rather than were dropped from some unknown hill existing in an unknown time.

We had come to see the Mesa Arch, a natural frame directing our attention to a commanding, sweeping view of the lowlands of Canyonlands National Park in Moab, Utah. Beyond the cliff, the next step of earth sat over one thousand feet below us. Canyonland's Island in the Sky mesa rises above the surrounding landscape like a pedestal. We followed the Colorado River from our home in Colorado's front range. Below us, it met at its confluence with the Green River. A single-lane road wound precariously down the face of cliffs, clinging to the narrow stone shelves. From this vantage, the world below seemed embossed, as if pressed into the earth.

Although the mesa beneath our feet felt solid, lending the assumption it would hold us steady above the earth one thousand feet below, the entire plateau is rather fragile, bound together by an intricate network of organisms. Despite the parched red dust exhaled from each step of our sandals, this mesa teems with life. Microscopic, biological soil crust webs itself across the miles of lofted land. This living ground cover makes life possible on the Island in the Sky. It creates a powerful web of fibers; a living net cinched around the earth. It is a resilient yet fragile protection against wind and water erosion.

At times it is difficult to picture the substance of our faith. Yet every moment we spend in prayer, each time we open God's Word, and every step we take toward him creates a living and active foundation. The same is true for your children. Never underestimate the power of one conversation or an hour spent out in creation. All of this creates a solid foundation from which their faith will grow.

Up there on the mesa, the microscopic web of life sustains the mesa and all who call it home, yet few will notice. Ignorant or unknowing steps off the path destroy the delicate system. The web is obliterated beneath sneaker treads. The same can be true of the creation-Creator connection. Many walk right past or trample on the evidence we have for God.

During the scientific revolution, when premodern times lapsed into modern times, many people began abandoning the assumption of a creator God. You can glimpse the wake of this in today's media, conversations, and curriculums. Reaching for a more tangible explanation for the world and our existence, they began seeking details and piecing together narratives—theories born of the soil and water—and abandoning anything that could not be proved in a glass beaker or test tube. Proving there is nothing new beneath the sun, the scientific revolution and shift to modern thinking reflected words written by the apostle Paul some 1,490 years before:

> For although they knew God, they did not honor him as God or give thanks to him, but they became futile in their thinking, and their foolish hearts were darkened. Claiming

to be wise, they became fools, and exchanged the glory of the immortal God for images resembling mortal man and birds and animals and creeping things.

Therefore God gave them up in the lusts of their hearts to impurity, to the dishonoring of their bodies among themselves, because they exchanged the truth about God for a lie *and worshiped and served the creature rather than the Creator*, who is blessed forever! Amen. (Rom. 1:21–25, emphasis added)

Society wanted the foundation without the cornerstone. Humanity wanted the mesa without the web of life holding it all together, and began to tread heavily on anything "supernatural." They unwound the Creator from the creation, and erosion began chipping away at the core. Anything that could not be touched, smelled, tasted, seen, heard, or experimented on was swept beneath a rug. This was the work of naturalism in modern thinking: to do away with anything supernatural or intangible.

This way of thinking has sprouted assumptions and behaviors that attempt to pollute our view of nature. Our children are growing up in a world that elevates nature on an unrealistic pedestal with a crumbling foundation. When we enjoy the mesa without regard to what holds it together—or absorb ourselves in nature with no thought given to its Designer and Sustainer—the conversation quickly loses depth.

You don't have to let your children grow up with this sterile understanding of the world around them. Without rhyme, reason, method, and intelligence, nature becomes lackluster. Instead, understanding creation as the wonderful expression of our artistic God, your children can fulfill their sense of purpose in enjoying and protecting what God has made. They can perceive the songs of creation as a worshipful chorus to the One who has plans for each of our lives. They can witness the earth's decay without fear or hopelessness but instead with an understanding that God is making all things new in his perfect timing.

There is a logical reason behind the instinctual pull we feel toward nature. We come from the ground. Genesis 2:7 says, "Then the Lord God formed the man of dust from the ground and breathed into his nostrils the breath of life, and the man became a living creature."

In his book *24/6*, Matthew Sleeth writes about humanity's starting point: "The word *Adam* is derived from the Hebrew word for the ground, dirt, earth, clay. God sculpts the ground and blows the breath of life into it. Despite all our cell membranes, electron transport chains, and protein enzymes, we are still inexorably part of the earth."[15]

If you have ever dug your fingers into wet, fragrant soil or warm sand, I bet you have felt this in your spirit. There is something inherently right about engaging with creation.

## Spending Time with the Artist

Imagine standing in front of the most famous painting in history. It's not a print; it's the real deal. You spend hours—no, days—studying each detail of that painting, the methods and mediums used to accomplish every stroke contributing to the final piece. It is a work of perfect design. After days spent staring at it, you're intimately familiar with it and could explain it very well to someone who only glimpses it passing by. Now imagine you know the artist, not only as an acquaintance, but as your closest friend. Would you look at the painting differently? Would you appreciate it more? Would you recognize the intent and inspiration for this piece? Would you notice more behind each detail than the passersby can see? This is how we come to appreciate art, care for it, and inspire others through it: by intimately knowing the artist behind it all.

The same is true for our connection with nature. As your children play outside, are they given ample time and opportunity to learn and appreciate the details of God's art and designs?

God has a vital role for nature in our lives. He created it in such a way as to draw us to himself. While my children pounce from one boulder to the next, chasing lizards and wonder, they are coming to know their Creator . . . or are they? It all depends on the discussions emanating from these experiences. It boils down to the narrative they'll adopt. We want to give them nature, but not half-served or with a hole-filled worldview. The question is this: Can we raise our children to be both Christ-followers and naturalists? It's a question I had to answer about myself first.

## What Is a Naturalist?

When you hear the words *naturalist* or *naturalism*, what comes to mind? Maybe it feels foreign and has little to no context. Maybe it feels a bit mystical and mysterious. Perhaps pictures of national park rangers or Smokey Bear with his "Only you can prevent forest fires!" mantra come to mind. As I researched the process to become a certified naturalist, I knew I needed to understand both the secular and biblical definitions of naturalism.

At first, the title "Master Naturalist" felt itchy. My passion for creation magnetized to the idea of becoming a naturalist. I wanted to acquire knowledge about creation that could then point others to God's glory. But as you might have discovered, naturalism has taken on a negative connotation in the evangelical world, and for a good reason. The following definitions lend these thoughts on the term:

1. Naturalism, in linguistic terms, means "a manner or technique of treating subject matter that presents, through volume of detail, *a deterministic view of human life and actions.*"
2. In the philosophical sphere, we find "the view of the world that takes account only of natural elements and forces, *excluding the supernatural or spiritual.*"
3. In the theological definition, we read, "the doctrine that all

religious truth is derived from a study of natural processes and not from revelation."[16]

I hesitated to pin that badge on my chest. Yet there are broader explanations as well, such as "a person who studies or is an expert in natural history, especially a zoologist or botanist,"[17] and "the depiction of the physical environment, especially landscape or the rural environment."[18] I gravitate toward this idea of becoming a teacher who shares about natural things.

I wanted my love for nature to lead me into detailed research and a well-rounded education about what God has made, and for that knowledge to drive my writing and teaching, that others may be "without excuse," like we read in Romans 1:20. So I changed my title to "master naturalist sharing the truth of God's Word through the wonders of his creation." Wordy? Yes. But also accurate.

You may abandon the term *naturalist* altogether for its connotations. But whatever way you describe this education, it is one we must not deny our children of or neglect for its importance. In nature, God has equipped us with a rich classroom teeming with robust materials that magnify his character and how he interacts with his children. By stepping outside—especially with a basic understanding and some context of the things God has made—we can show our children who God is and how he cares for his creation.

It is essential for our children's understanding and worldview to reconnect the dots between creation and Creator. We can read our children Bible stories from the womb or adoption day until their eighteenth birthday. Still, we must also give them sure and steadfast evidence for their faith. We can show our children that there is tangible evidence of life discovered throughout nature, science, and history, and tie that knowledge to biblical truths. We can strengthen that web of life, securing together their foundation of faith so that no matter who comes trampling around, it will not succumb to erosion. We can familiarize our children with the nature narratives strung throughout Scripture and offer them vivid imagery and experiences into which they can anchor their beliefs. We can redeem naturalist and infuse the discussion of nature with the depth and breadth of Scripture.

It's time to take down the "tread carefully" signs around your children's faith. There will be no need for them as you equip your children with evidence supporting what they believe. They will know—from the birds' songs, ways of the wind, tree's roots, and mountain's contours, all supported by the biblical narrative—that there is an intelligent mind behind every design.

Against the backdrop of their natural education, our children can nod knowingly at passages like Colossians 1:16–17: "For by him all things were created, in heaven and on earth, visible and invisible, whether thrones or dominions or rulers or authorities—all things were created through him and for him. And he is before all things," and, just like the microscopic life-forms holding together the Island in the Sky mesa, "in him all things hold together."

Picture again Galileo and Kepler turning the telescope toward the skies. Just as they recognized the telescope's potential to help better understand the cosmos, you can view nature—interpreted through biblical truth—as a tool to introduce your children to new discoveries about God. Looking all around—and up—may we too echo the prayer of King David in Psalm 8:1, 3–4.

> O LORD, our Lord,
>> how majestic is your name in all the earth!
> You have set your glory above the heavens . . .
>
> When I look at your heavens, the work of your fingers,
>> the moon and the stars, which you have set in place,
> what is man that you are mindful of him,
>> and the son of man that you care for him?

You might be surprised by how simple and fun it is to reconnect the dots between creation and Creator. It only requires time outdoors and in God's Word. The connections and synthesis between his Word and world come naturally. As your children develop habits of noticing God's hand in creation, they will draw conclusions for the hard questions of faith. Doubts will dissolve as your children discover a resilient web of life around what they believe.

## Step Outside

God wants your children to discover him in nature. It's why he left so many hints about who he is, much like fingerprints embossed on everything he's made. Then he tucked curiosity into your children's hearts and intelligence in their minds. Your children are naturally inclined and equipped to see God in creation. Your job is simply to explore alongside them through God's Word and world. Through the lens of nature, you and your children will come to a deeper understanding of God's qualities and characteristics, and how he interacts with us, his children. By reconnecting the dots between creation and Creator, your children's faith will gain substance and confidence.

### See Nature in the Bible
- Read to your children Genesis 15:5–6. Ask what they think Abram saw that night. Then ask them what they believe Abram would have seen if he had a telescope.
- Read your children Psalm 8:3–4. Explain to them that God hung every star in space, even those we'll never know about. He knows their number and has named each one (Ps. 147:4). Assure your children that in the same way, God knows our names and cares about us deeply.
- Is there a time from your childhood or recent past that nature took your breath away or left you in awe of God? Share that story

with your children so they can see that you also are affected by God's wonderful world.

## See God in Nature

- Plan one night in the upcoming month to allow your children to stay up late or wake them during the night. Take them outside to watch the night sky. Remember to check the weather to make sure the sky will be clear. If necessary, drive away from city lights for a better view.
- Read to your children Psalm 19:1: "The heavens declare the glory of God, and the sky above proclaims his handiwork." Tell them the word *declare* can mean "celebrate." Ask them how we too can celebrate God's beauty. If they need some ideas, consider drawing a picture or writing a poem or song about the night sky, or saying a prayer to thank God for everything he has made.

— 3 —

# Creation Groans . . . Until It Sings

*One learns that the world, though made, is yet being*
*made; that this is still the morning of creation; that*
*mountains long conceived are now being born, channels*
*traced for coming rivers, basins hollowed for lakes.*

JOHN MUIR

CLIMATE CHANGE CAN BE A tricky subject to broach with your children. Perhaps you grew up hearing about a warming earth and melting ice caps and viewed it through a haze of conspiracy. Maybe it has induced nervousness when you hear about temperatures rising, droughts elongating, and species of creatures going extinct at alarming rates. Like when you live in a home and things break, flood, catch fire, or you experience any other home disaster, it feels personal and costly—even scary. How much more so, then, on the scale of planet Earth. Although we cannot answer every climate change question for our children, we can equip them with a biblical lens through which to view these issues. As they (and we) gain a clearer understanding of God's plan for Earth and our roles in that plan, we shed fear and confusion and equip our kids with a faith resilient against any drought, flood, or fire—including the ones I've experienced near our home in Colorado.

"This is a unique hillside." My fellow volunteer with our city's natural areas department pointed to the sparse eastern slope of Green Ridge.

On this day, I was not a volunteer but a student alongside my nine-year-old son.

"We're not exactly sure why it has not reforested after the fire twenty years ago," my colleague explained. "A lot of research has been done on this hillside and a few similar to it. They think the fire burned so hot that it sterilized the soil. The main reason is it's just too hot and dry. Nothing can regrow."

The slanted landscape contradicts what we know about wildfires and their redeeming factor: that in the aftermath, the landscape regrows and flourishes. In healthy soil, the land regenerates itself. Vibrant pink fireweed blooms like a decorative rug rolled out over the blackened forest floor. Some plants even require wildfire, like those with serotinous seeds. A serotinous seed cannot open or help the plant reproduce except through extreme wildfire temperatures.

New growth in the fire's wake provides lush carpets of native grasses, wildflowers, and trees. This reforestation after fire reflects Romans 5:3–5: "We rejoice in our sufferings, knowing that suffering produces endurance, and endurance produces character, and character produces hope, and hope does not put us to shame, because God's love has been poured into our hearts through the Holy Spirit who has been given to us." Hardships are perfect soil for growing resilient faith that "does not put us to shame." It is an enduring faith supported by what we see in nature.

But then we have Green Ridge. Soil matters when it comes to regrowth, and Green Ridge's barren expanse is a stark example of wildfire with no glory and little purpose. The fire's aftermath feels futile, like a tragedy.

The fire two decades ago claimed only a portion of the ridge. The remainder of the natural area—a historic homestead and miles of trails winding through tall grasses and ponderosa pines—is an oasis at the city's outskirts. A week after our class, I returned with all four of my children. We explored the historic barns and set up in the park shelter to read and paint. Rock wrens danced in the blooming yellow rabbitbrush all around us.

Eleven days later, the entire area caught fire again. From our home a few miles east, I stared at an aerial image on my phone showing the barns still standing but the surrounding grasslands blackened and smoldering. We never thought, when a fire was ignited two months before, far up in one of our favorite canyons, that it would come this close to home. The thought never crossed our minds that it would become the largest fire in Colorado's written history. We were heading into months of thick, choking, smoke-filled days. On afternoons when the wind picked up and stoked the flames, massive plumes or "pyrocumulus clouds" of towering smoke would build and fan out over the entire front range. The fire was creating its own weather.

We witnessed stretches of days when the sky was bruised black and orange. Ash and scorched pine needles—remnants of our favorite trails—fell like snow around us.

Snow—*real* snow—is what we desperately needed, but it was summer. I'd learned through my naturalist training that rain was not our best defense against this fire. Too much rain too soon after a fire floods our rivers with debris and can create a near toxic environment.

On the other hand, snow would take a gentler approach of blanketing the burned areas and suffocating the flames. Ironically, a record early snowfall was in the forecast. Saturday of Labor Day weekend, the fire reared up and roared. It grew from where it had stood steady at thirty-four thousand acres for weeks to over ninety-thousand acres throughout the holiday weekend. It was the first of many of our apocalyptic-style stretches of days. We drove to a nearby reservoir and looked out over the lake. The water was a bright orange reflection of the sky above.

"Tell them to remember this." An older gentleman stood beside me and nodded toward my five-year-old son. "They'll never again see anything like it." He was here during the High Park Fire eight years prior, he told me. That fire had burned for three weeks, devouring eighty-seven thousand acres.

The fire I was staring at had already burned for a month. Before it finished, it would claim 208,913 acres.[1] I hope he's right. I don't want my kids to see this again. Yet from my naturalist studies, I know how necessary it is. This land aches to burn. Throughout the earth's history, wildfire has been an ecological necessity for restoring landscapes.

But if you have ever experienced a wildfire, you know how threatening it feels. It's difficult to believe something so extreme can at the same time be necessary for new life.

Where I live, it's not only natural but also highly political. Journalist Heather Hansen explains a shift that took place in 1995 regarding how we think about wildfire. "The Federal Wildland Fire Management Policy officially confirmed that, 'Wildland fire will be used to protect, maintain, and enhance resources and, as nearly as possible, be allowed to function in its natural ecological role.'"[2]

Fire's job is to purge, clean, and restore.

We know the land needs it, but more and more homeowners are choosing to live in areas vulnerable to fire. Thousands of people build into the WUI (Wildland Urban Interface), where urban neighborhoods press into wild areas. In the WUI, fires are not a matter of if, but when. Watching the Cameron Peak wildfire burning close to our home, I couldn't know it then, but the following year, another fire would burn just south of us. Two days before the new year, while kids were still oohing and awing over their Christmas gifts, the Marshall Fire would ignite in a grassy field. High winds would kick up the flames, and it would devour 1,083 residential homes within hours. Living in the WUI is not without risk.

Observing the Cameron Peak Fire, I bade the gentleman on the ridge goodbye. We packed our kids into the SUV and continued north up to the radio towers. We visit this obscure spot regularly to view the mountains. On that day, another car was parked in the often-deserted gravel parkway. We stood silently, watching smoke travel along peaks. Orange plumes rose at the front of the wall of smoke, devouring trees. My husband spoke with the owner of the other car.

"My wife and daughters evacuated yesterday. They're at a hotel down in town." The man's eyes did not divert from the blaze. "That's our home down there, we bought it last year. We have chickens." He pointed a quarter mile west of where we stood.

"This snow needs to come soon," he said, desperation lacing his words. He explained that if the clouds didn't let loose by tomorrow, the fire would reach where we were standing. His house would be gone.

In my own home the following day, I opened the blinds to a miracle. A blanket of summer snow. The fire-affected areas received up to fourteen inches. I called the kids over and read to them from Job 38:22–23, "Have you entered the storehouses of the snow, and have you seen the storehouses of the hail, which I have reserved for a time of distress . . . ?" (NASB).

Snow fell for nearly two days. The fire did not reach the radio towers.

## Planet Earth Has an End Date

Have you ever experienced a gracious pause from God amid the fires of life? At times he inserts an interlude in our troubles to allow us to rest and to reassess—to remember he is good and in control. Our early snowfall was one of those gracious pauses. Although it did not claim complete victory over the fire (we would learn in coming weeks just how beastly this blaze was), it did provide the firefighters and homeowners in the foothills the reprieve for which they were desperate. We could all inhale the fresh air, even if only for a moment. Firefighters stepped back, assessed the fire's behavior and trajectory, and prepared for what was to come. It was still summer, and we were still in drought and high fire danger.

In the following weeks, the Cameron Peak Fire developed an erratic and unpredictable cadence of standing up and laying down; inhaling and exhaling; teasing, relenting, rushing, running. Neighbors a few miles from us were told to evacuate. We wondered if our turn would come.

"It's this drought," everyone was saying. The warming earth. Trapped gasses. Climate change. This was our fourth summer in Colorado. We had limited experience or context for the local history and weather patterns. But we knew it was hot and dry, much more so than our previous summers. I wanted to get at the truth of the matter. Were drought and fire to become our new normal, or was this another one of Earth's patterns, bound to slacken and relent with time? With the fire a ridge away, we suffered from a nearsighted state of alarm. But is wildfire more stable than we realize? Could it be a cyclical system of destruction and regeneration?

If you're like me, you want to offer your children more than a shoulder shrug when they come with questions about climate change. Our kids hear it regularly: "The earth is warming up," and without context, this information can cause alarm and anxiety in children. As the wildfire burned near our home, my kids watched the sunset behind our mountains give way to the eerie orange glow of the blaze creeping toward town. Living in drought and feeling the heat of approaching flames, it was difficult not to dramatize and exaggerate what was happening. It's important in the heat of disaster or threat that we take a step back to gather the facts. Instead of reacting in fear, we can show our kids what it looks like to remain calm and take a hard look at what is actually happening, then make a wise plan.

Science points to increasing temperatures on our planet. From 1880 to 1980, the combined land and ocean temperature rose at an average rate of 0.13 degrees Fahrenheit (0.08 degrees Celsius) each decade. Since 1981, that rate of increasing temperature has nearly doubled.[3] We see a significant correlation between the earth's temperature rising alongside our technological and industrial advancements. The world does indeed seem to be warming up. This also aligns with our biblical understanding, however. Second Peter 3:10 states plainly how this planet expires: "But the day of the Lord will come like a thief. The heavens will disappear with a roar; the elements will be destroyed by fire, and the earth and everything done in it will be laid bare" (NIV).

"Like a thief" assumes this event will be a surprise. But could it be possible that the warming of our planet, set in motion by humanity's activities, paves the way for the earth's expiration? In the beginning, the earth was "subject to futility" and "destruction." Could this have set the stage for that day when fire will claim our planet? By this theory, global warming fits within our biblical narrative. Yet we must not exaggerate the speed or urgency of this matter. Doing so only breeds fear. From the unbeliever's standpoint, this terrible reality evokes great anxiety: our home planet is burning up and leading to the extinction of our species. We don't need to be afraid, though, when we understand God's plan and rest secure in his salvation and our eternity with him. We know Earth's days are numbered. As you explain to your children that, because this world is broken by sin, God is working to make all things new, they can gain confidence and peace in light of God's plans.

The rate at which the earth seems to be warming up is another example of God's sovereign protection. Melissa Cain Travis explains that the earth's atmosphere is a perfect example of a planet finely tuned to support both life and fire. She writes: "Our atmosphere has just under 21 percent oxygen, and for every 1 percent increase in this level there would be a 70 percent increase in the probability of wildfires. On the other hand, if oxygen levels were lower, large land-dwellers like humans wouldn't flourish."[4]

A slight downward turn on the oxygen dial, and we would fail to thrive or live at all. A tiny dialing up, and the planet would be consumed by fire. As I experience wildfires near my home, I can say with certainty that a 70 percent increase in fires would be devastating.

Those worshiping creation rather than Creator, or, to a lesser degree, depending on Earth to sustain their lives, are in for disappointment. When nature fails to save them, when they look to the stars to tell them their futures, when they flock to the forest for the peace only the Maker of the forest can give, or they ask science for all the answers to their soul-deep questions, nature will come up short. Just like us. Because nature, like us, is broken. It is decaying. We gain an alarming image of this decay in Isaiah 24:1, 3–6:

> Behold, the LORD will empty the earth and make it desolate,
>     and he will twist its surface and scatter its inhabitants . . .
> The earth shall be utterly empty and utterly plundered;
>     for the LORD has spoken this word.
>
> The earth mourns and withers;
>     · the world languishes and withers;
>     the highest people of the earth languish.
> The earth lies defiled
>     under its inhabitants;
> for they have transgressed the laws,
>     violated the statutes,
>     broken the everlasting covenant.
> Therefore a curse devours the earth,
>     and its inhabitants suffer for their guilt;

therefore the inhabitants of the earth are scorched,
and few men are left.

As the curse devours our planet, creation is simultaneously waiting for all things to be made new. We read about this in Revelation
21:1, 5: "Then I saw a new heaven and a new earth, for the first
heaven and the first earth had passed away, and the sea was no more.
. . . And he who was seated on the throne said, 'Behold, I am making
all things new.'"

When our children see the earth's decay, and as they hear creation
groaning for newness and our Maker, their attention will be lifted
not to the galaxies but further beyond to the One who strung each
galaxy together.

We can reassure our children with facts and truth. Maybe you
can't understand every nuance in the discussion of climate change,
but you can turn your ear toward it. You can listen to what is being
said, then measure it against what we know from God's Word.

## Cursed Is the Ground

God's plan for restoration and regeneration offers us steadfast hope
in the face of decay and destruction around us.

Ecclesiastes 3:11 tells us, "He has made everything beautiful in
its time. Also, he has put eternity into man's heart." He tucked the
concept of eternity into our hearts. The assurance of his restoration
carries us forward with an eternal perspective. As you help your
children align their thoughts with God's thoughts through the study
of his Word, this eternal perspective will extinguish fear and grant
confidence.

Contrasting the earth's decay, we can point them to God's everlast-
ing truth in Isaiah 40:8, "The grass withers, the flower fades, but the
word of our God will stand forever." As our children grapple with the
idea and associated fears of an expiring planet, we can assure them

that although creation is broken, our Creator is preparing something far greater, and he will not fail. When my kids ask me what heaven will be like, I often tell them I believe it will be like this earth, only how it was supposed to be, as it was portrayed in the garden of Eden. It won't be broken. It will be everything beautiful without any of the bad.

Hebrews 1:10–12 says:

> You, Lord, laid the foundation of the earth in the beginning,
>   and the heavens are the work of your hands;
> they will perish, but you remain;
>   they will all wear out like a garment,
> like a robe you will roll them up,
>   like a garment they will be changed.
> But you are the same,
>   and your years will have no end.

Let's return to our foundation verse in Romans 1:20: "For his invisible attributes, namely, his eternal power and divine nature, have been clearly perceived, ever since the creation of the world, in the things that have been made. So they are without excuse." Tracing this verse seven chapters later, we find a glimpse of nature's trajectory. In Romans 8:19–22 we read:

> For the creation waits with eager longing for the revealing of the sons of God. For the creation was subjected to futility, not willingly, but because of him who subjected it, in hope that the creation itself will be set free from its bondage to corruption and obtain the freedom of the glory of the children of God. For we know that the whole creation has been groaning together in the pains of childbirth until now.

Let's break down this passage and see what it's saying about Earth's lifespan:

1. Nature was subjected to futility. The Greek word used here for *futility* can mean "depravity," "devoid of truth," and "frailty." This took place in the garden of Eden, when sin set the stage for history's progression. We read in Genesis 3:17, "Cursed is the ground because of you."

2. Although God subjected the earth to futility, it resulted from Adam and Eve's actions. This would set a pattern. The land was now enslaved to corruption or, at the roots of the Greek definition, "destruction" and "perishing."

3. Now enslaved, creation awaits eagerly—even with audible groans—for liberation. Paul, the author of Romans, parallels this to our waiting for freedom from our sinful state, for the full glory believers will enjoy with Christ.

4. Creation groans as if in childbirth pains. As a mother enduring nearly unbearable labor pain, nature endures in hope and assurance of what is coming.

On the note of Earth's gradual decay, Aldo Leopold used the term *land sickness*. Referring to disappearing species and dramatic imbalances in our ecosystems, he said these events are "occurring too frequently to be dismissed as normal evolutionary events."[5]

Cursed is the ground.

## It Is Still the Morning of Creation

This is the hope you can offer your children: God has made the only cure for this land sickness! Through the sacrifice of his Son, Jesus, we can be made new and experience perfect and eternal life with him. This broken earth is not all there is.

While traveling across Alaska and noticing the landscape's decay, the late naturalist John Muir proposed, "This is still the morning of creation."[6] As an early environmentalist and believer in the creator God, Muir took a particular interest in glaciers. Although he noted their observable melt, he also highlighted the life-giving effects of glacial melt. Valleys below, lush with green grass and arrayed in wildflowers, showed him that even the diminishing glaciers created something new, like a forest of juvenile trees after a fire. Even the groans of creation join into the anthem of praise to God who makes all things new.

I saw this firsthand in the Snowy Range of Wyoming. On a particularly smoky day during our wildfire season, our family drove several hours north to find fresh air. Wandering the alpine tundra across the Medicine Bow Mountains, our children skipped off trails to slide on their bellies like penguins down snow-packed hills. Below them, soggy grass and vibrant wildflowers created living gaps between rock and ice; the decay of one created life for another. Our God is not wasteful.

Although Romans 8 shows us the trajectory of nature, it doesn't offer a timeline. Only God knows the number of turns on its axis this planet will take and when exactly he'll make all things new. Earlier, in 2 Peter 3:10, we read about the earth being swallowed by flames. The passage does not end there, however. Instead, it shows us the implications for our lives:

> But the day of the Lord will come like a thief. The heavens will disappear with a roar; the elements will be destroyed by fire, and the earth and everything done in it will be laid bare.

> Since everything will be destroyed in this way, what kind of people ought you to be? You ought to live holy and godly lives as you look forward to the day of God and speed its coming. That day will bring about the destruction of the heavens by fire, and the elements will melt in the heat. But in keeping with

his promise we are looking forward to a new heaven and a new earth, where righteousness dwells. (vv. 10–13 NIV)

May our waiting not be idle but active. May our kids listen to creation's anthem and eagerly watch as God makes all things new.

## The Laws of Nature Bow at His Command

The changing earth does not catch us off guard because we, as believers, recognize the natural decay as God-ordained, something for which God has a plan. Creation's groans are a foreshadow of restoration.

Another assurance in the biblical narrative is that creation is always subject to God. Your children can build their faith on the foundation of God's sovereignty—he has full control. In Job 38, we overhear God speaking to Job from out of a whirlwind. His questions to Job reveal God's power over every element in the universe. God presses Job to consider things like:

- "Where were you when I laid the foundation of the earth? Tell me, if you have understanding. Who determined its measurements—surely you know! Or who stretched the line upon it?" (vv. 4–5).
- "Have you commanded the morning since your days began, and caused the dawn to know its place . . . ?" (v. 12).
- "Can you bind the chains of the Pleiades or loose the cords of Orion?" (v. 31).
- "Can you lift up your voice to the clouds, that a flood of waters may cover you? Can you send forth lightnings, that they may go and say to you, 'Here we are'?" (vv. 34–35).

Job 38–39 provides a run-on dialogue of God declaring his dominion over earth and sky. Even human-caused destruction—whether it be campers neglecting to douse their campfire, or trash tossed into the ocean—does not escape God's sovereignty. He created nature to serve humanity. In the Old Testament, we see this truth materialized in miracles. Consider the two examples below.

### Israel Walks Across Dry Ground

In Exodus 14, God used nature to carve an escape route for Israel, liberating them from Egyptian slavery. Moses assured the masses of refugees in verse 13, "Fear not, stand firm, and see the salvation of the LORD, which he will work for you today. For the Egyptians whom you see today, you shall never see again." God then instructed Moses, "Tell the people of Israel to go forward. Lift up your staff, and stretch out your hand over the sea and divide it, that the people of Israel may go through the sea on dry ground" (vv. 15–16).

Throughout their escape, God positioned pillars of cloud to lead and protect them; then he split open the depths of the sea. The Israelites stepped onto sea bottom. Their sandals did not sink or suction in muddy earth saturated with salt water. Instead, they walked across on dry land hemmed in by walls of seawater. Once they had safely passed through, the waters rushed back to their place at God's instruction, swallowing the enemy Egyptians.

### The Sun Stands Still

In Joshua 10, God bent the laws of nature to give his people victory in battle. In verse 8, God assured Joshua as he headed into action, "Do not fear them, for I have given them into your hands." In verse 11 we see God using Earth's systems to give favor to the Israelite team, "The LORD threw down large stones from heaven on them as far as Azekah, and they died." More impressive than a hailstorm was the event that followed. Emboldened by God's faithfulness, Joshua declared in verse 12, "Sun, stand still at Gibeon, and moon, in the Valley of Aijalon." For an entire day, the sun stood still until Israel claimed victory over its enemies. Verse 14 summarizes, "There has been no day like it before or since, when the LORD heeded the voice of a man, for the LORD fought for Israel."

Creation is composed in a mathematical and orderly manner. Yet when it comes to caring for his children, our Creator can bend the norms and even the laws of nature. He is, after all, the One who wrote those laws. He can suspend natural order for a unique and miraculous instance.

## God Works Within His Means and Outside Our Understanding

God can also work within the laws of nature—to an extent our scientific discoveries are yet unaware of—to perform what *looks* to us like a miracle but fits within the confines of time, space, and math.

Although we have biblical accounts backed by historical and scientific findings, miracles are not God's usual way of conducting business. But perhaps he has created laws within nature we haven't yet discovered, ones which very well may look like miracles to us. For example, when God created light, he worked into those laws the potential of a rainbow. The first mention of a rainbow is in Genesis 9—eleven generations into humanity's history. The Bible does not plainly say whether this was the first instance of a rainbow, or if there were prior rainbows, and this is when God marked the rainbow's significance as a sign of his promise. If it was indeed the first rainbow, he had written its potential way back at creation, then revealed it generations later. Likewise, we have yet to explore most of the ocean. As of this writing, less than 25 percent of its floor has been mapped by sonar technology.[7] And that is only the seabed! What have we yet to discover between its surface and floor? "Here is the sea, great and wide," we read in Psalm 104:25, "which teems with creatures innumerable, living things both small and great." With around 75 percent of our ocean floor unmapped, how many oceanic wonders might we be yet unaware of?

St. Augustine wrote, "So miracle is not contrary to nature, but only to what we know of nature."[8]

Consider everything we're missing! Might there be more to creation than we perceive? Perhaps God has withheld some of nature's potential and will reveal it when Earth's end draws near. Whatever methods he chooses, it proves his sovereignty over all things. Nature bows at his voice.

As our children become familiar with these biblical accounts of God's power over nature, security replaces fear. When they hear about wildfires, tornadoes, tsunamis, hurricanes, drought, or earthquakes, they can return to what they know is true: God is in control, and he has an ultimate plan. He is at this moment making all things new.

I witnessed this in my own children's faith in the three months that our fire burned. Whatever each day brought, whether choking smoke, orange skies, news of new evacuations, or piles of ash in our driveway, we had the opportunity to grow. As gold purified by flame, our faith was tested. Impurities of fear and anxiety were purged.

We spoke with our kids often about fire's natural place in the ecosystem and how God uses it to restore the land. In each conversation, we aimed to turn the focus to a God who is loving, powerful, and near. In every hardship, you can point your children to a God who is ever-present. He does not disregard your children's fears. Instead, the One who commands the seas and skies bends low to us, his children, and turns our attention to his hope and truth.

## He Is Making All Things New

The sneaky thing about a fire is that the danger is not over when the final ember cools. Finally, in November, the fire laid down under a heavy blanket of snow, but more damage was to come. After the quiet respite of winter, spring showers wreaked havoc on our rivers and canyons. With trees and understory burned away, rainfall had no foliage to soak into, resulting in devastating floods.

We drove up to witness the damage after one particularly tragic flood. My stomach sank. Less than a year before, we'd watched flames devour our favorite hiking spots along this route. The canyon hardly had a chance to take a breath after the catastrophe, and here was another calamity. My husband slowed as we passed the worst of the wreckage. Rescue dogs sporting blaze-orange vests sniffed at the mountains of rubble. Workers carefully shuffled through heaps of debris, searching for missing people.

The river cleared up as we passed the worst of the flash flood area. There was still mud everywhere, but no more fridges, box fans, or other everyday artifacts strewn about the water.

"A bear!" My husband's exclamation broke into my heavy, tangled thoughts. He pulled the car over.

On the opposite riverbank stood a young, cinnamon black bear. He remained for a few minutes watching the water before noticing our attention and retreating up the hillside. Less than a mile downriver, volunteers searched through rubble. Less than a mile upriver, the woods were charred black from fire. Yet here, amid so much devastation, stood a young black bear that had somehow weathered the harshest of conditions. The color of hope looks a little bit mud brown with cinnamon highlights and a white patch on his chest.

There is a building anthem composed of underlying groans. Quickly and stunningly, it is transforming into a profound melody. Psalm 66:4 proclaims, "All the earth worships you and sings praises to you; they sing praises to your name." This word *earth* not only alludes to humanity. It is the same word used in Genesis 1:1, "In the beginning, God created the heavens and the *earth*" (emphasis added). It refers to land, soil, field, and wilderness.

All of nature is singing. If we listen carefully to this chorus, we'll hear a promise of new life.

## Step Outside

When your children walk through life's uncertainties, they can place their hope in a God who is the bringer of new life. Not only is God completely in control of every circumstance, but he is actively working toward our good and his glory. When your children ask questions about climate change or Earth's decay, be honest with them when you do not know the answers. Assure them that although we can't know the answer or outcome of all these issues, the Bible tells us with certainty that God is in control, and he has good plans.

You can use the example of a wildfire and serotinous seeds found in some pine trees and eucalyptus. You can even find a pinecone or purchase a eucalyptus stem from a floral shop to use as a visual. Explain how fire is the only way for these plants to grow, and sometimes God uses hard things to bring new life and grow our faith stronger.

### See Nature in the Bible

- Read your children Isaiah 43:19 in the NCV translation: "Look at the new thing I am going to do. It is already happening. Don't you see it? I will make a road in the desert and rivers in the dry land."
- Explain to your children that in life we will go through many wilderness and desert places where things feel hard and dangerous. Ask them what difficult things they have recently walked through, and how they see God working through those hard things to grow their faith.
- Ask your children if they are afraid of anything that they hear about happening on Earth, such as natural disasters. Pray with them and help them lay those fears in God's hands and trust him for protection. Here is a sample prayer you can use: "Dear God, thank you for being in control. Sometimes scary things happen on Earth, but we know that you rule over creation. You

made everything on Earth, and nature listens to your voice. We know things in nature are broken because of sin, but you are still in control. Help me to not live in fear, but to trust that even in hard things you are at work bringing new life. Amen."

### See God in Nature

Take your children on a scavenger hunt for new life. Walk along a trail or through a natural area with a notebook. Write down or draw every hint of new life you can see:

- Bird nests or eggs
- Green shoots of plants
- Baby trees
- Buds on branches
- Aquatic plants in ponds
- Tadpoles
- Insect eggs on leaves

This activity is best to do in spring. But God is constantly working toward new life throughout the year.

In summer, you can talk about the cycles of wildflowers. Flowers grow, bloom, then die, making way for new flowers. Their colors and scents tell a story of new life throughout the season.

In fall, you can share how trees shed their leaves in anticipation of a new year. They let go of the past to welcome the future. You can read Philippians 3:13–14 (NCV): "There is one thing I always do. Forgetting the past and straining toward what is ahead, I keep trying to reach the goal and get the prize for which God called me through Christ to the life above."

In winter, you can take a walk and talk about how nature is getting ready for spring. Perennial plants, which come back every year, are strengthening their roots beneath the frozen soil. Snow is soaking the ground with water to help baby flowers come out in spring. Mama animals are readying to give birth. Birds are planning their nest designs. Explain to your children that God is always creating, and he loves to bring new life to nature and our hearts!

— 4 —

# Nurturing Contagious Curiosity in Your Children

*Children are born with all the wonder they will ever*
*need. Our job is not to take it away.*

AINSLEY ARMENT

DO YOU CONSIDER YOURSELF A naturally curious person? As a child, were you drawn to the mysteries of nature and compelled to find answers for its many questions? Maybe you feel your curiosity has become stale with the passing of time. Whatever level of interest you currently have about natural things, curiosity is a trained habit. As you develop your own natural interests, time with your children will become all the more meaningful as together you discover God in creation.

I have not always been deeply intrigued by wildlife. My children, unbeknownst to them, have tapped it back into me. What time has sapped away, they have rejuvenated in my spirit. They teach me to sit in the dirt, examine a dragonfly's flight, consider a beetle's pace and direction, and close my eyes to filter out everything but a birdsong.

Their curiosity has taught me to care. It has awakened in me a deep appreciation for what God has made. This respect for life and fascination with creation is what woke me in the middle of the night on March 20, 2021, the first day of spring.

"Eryn, come quick." My husband's voice pulled me from my dreams. His urgent tone told me our chicks were hatching, and I wasn't ready.

"Can you go get the bin from the garage?" I asked him as I rushed downstairs and into our kitchen. The incubator had sat dead-still for over three weeks. I'd given up. I knew we'd messed something up. I'd let the humidity drop too low. I'd opened the top too many times, trying to "candle" the eggs above a spotlight, looking for red veins developing, searching for life.

But I was wrong. Peering into the dark plastic top of the incubator, through the water droplets of humidity, two tiny Coturnix quail stumbled around their unhatched siblings. They gave no thought to other chicks still tucked in fragile shells, waiting for their time. Instead, our first two hatchlings pressed their tiny bodies up on twine-thin legs, fell, tried again, tumbled, and knocked the sleepy eggs to and fro.

Grayson placed a bin on the counter. I quickly filled it with woodchips to create a cozy habitat. Then I gently lifted the incubator lid and slid my fingers beneath the feet of a chick. Gently, I lifted and placed her near my face for just a moment before relocating her to the bin. She peeped incessantly, sounding her alarm until I set the second chick beside her.

I watched them for a few minutes, then reluctantly retired back to bed. A maternal instinct urged me to stay awake, but I knew this was much different than the four nights I'd labored my babies into the world. This time, there was nothing for me to do. I left nature to itself and curled up beneath my comforter.

The next morning, one more chick was rolling around in the incubator.

"Boys, come here!" I yelled upstairs.

I lifted the incubator lid, and they stared, completely enthralled. Another egg was moving, starting, trying, preparing to hatch. Tears welled in my eyes.

We watched throughout the morning as several more chicks hatched. Each one began by "pipping" a tiny hole in the egg from inside. From that hole, they perforated a straight line around the circumference of the egg, like a page from an easy-tear coloring book. Once the perforation was complete, the chick pressed with all its tiny pent-up might until its legs separated the two halves and the baby emerged. It is one of the closest things to a miracle I've ever seen. It drew my thoughts toward the careful designs God has given us in nature. He tucks into these tiny birds an innate knowledge of how to enter the world. They understand the job before them and perform it dutifully.

"Mama," my three-year-old daughter said as she peered into the bin, "I hear them singing." I knew this will be a sound of her childhood. Her mind recorded the chicks' excited chirping, marking it as relevant and meaningful among her memories. It's when she first witnessed life emerging. Hope hatching.

Our quail broods' arrival was not the only excitement of the day. When five chicks had emerged, family from Chicago arrived after driving through the night. My brother-in-law, his wife, and their three sons came through the door. We had not seen them in months. After hugs and hellos, we ushered them to the quail bin. Just as with my children hours earlier, I watched as my nephews were thoroughly entranced by the wonder of new life.

Our family began settling in and unpacking while my boys lugged tables and heavy bins outside. The containers were packed with fossils unearthed from our neighborhood. A year before, this development was a prairie. It pains me to know the habitat that was sacrificed for our home. But I find joy in how my children have preserved and honored the past.

"There are fossils here," the builder told us the first time we walked through the house. There was no yard yet, no fence, the home newly finished.

"We found tons of them when we were digging foundations. If your kids look for them, they'll probably find some."

And they did. Within the first weeks of moving in, we had a respectable museum claiming corners of our home. The boys teamed up to carry massive rocks decorated in clamshell fossils. The museum quickly spilled out over into the yard, where rocks too large to carry in stood as statues from another time. Prairie dog skulls became an exhibit all by themselves. One afternoon, our youngest son rushed home from the nearby creek he was playing in with his big brothers to show us his treasure: a complete ammonite fossil the size of his palm. We could observe the entire spiral shell. I'd never seen anything like it outside a museum.

The boys' cousins quickly joined in the morning's work as if they had been part of the planning committee for weeks. They set up displays across our front sidewalk. A week earlier, my sons hand-delivered flyers to the entire neighborhood:

Celebrate the first day of Spring at the outdoor museum! Come experience geodes, crystals, and fossils! From near and far, even in our own neighborhood!

The boys finished arranging their displays and sat, waiting anxiously and wondering if anyone would come. I carefully brought out our bonus exhibit, a chirping bin of thumb-sized baby birds beneath their heat lamp. Ten minutes passed. My oldest son lowered in his seat. Then, cars began arriving. Our oldest son directed museum-goers to his hand-drawn map of the neighborhood, pointing to where each fossil on the table was discovered. One neighbor brought a gift of fossils from his childhood.

"I've been holding onto these for a long time," he explained, nostalgia dripping from his voice, but no regret or resignation. "It's time to pass them along."

Another neighbor brought a massive encyclopedia on fossils. "My name and address are in the front cover," she explained, "whenever you're done with it, just bring it back anytime with your mom. I can show you our fossil collection as well."

I stood back, astounded, watching my boys interacting with neighbors. I saw the sparkle in the adults' eyes, watching children with the same curiosity they themselves once held. Have you ever felt this spark of nostalgia and joy in watching your children play with nature? It restores our own intrigue with God's world. It's rejuvenating to watch children spending their days exploring nature.

Your children have this potential inside of them to point others to God's creations. It's a wonderful way to share his truth and gospel! Sometimes they only need a little bit of permission and inspiration. Your budding curiosity will fuel theirs. As they see you becoming excited about rocks, trees, birds, insects, weather, or whatever other natural thing piques your interest, they will follow, and they'll bring others along for the adventure.

## Curiosity Is Contagious

Has someone's excitement for something ever ignited your own interests? Perhaps you were unaware or uninterested in a topic until someone shared their passion and it compelled you to learn more. This was my experience with the black-footed ferret.

The night was black, nearly untouched by the city lights an hour south. My husband and I, and ten other class participants, walked silently across the dark prairie. Late September air swept the prairie grasses; brittle desert brush crunched beneath our boots velcroed tight under snake guards. Our headlamps sliced through the night, rebounding off rocks. Taking turns with spotlights, we scanned the landscape, searching for an emerald-green reflection. I hoped it was not a lost cause.

"Their eyes are how we find them," our natural areas director explained. Together we were leading a program about the black-footed ferrets.

Upon moving to Colorado, when my husband told me ferrets are a native species here, I didn't believe him. I was familiar with the domesticated pet ferrets I grew up with and couldn't imagine their wild relative bounding across our desert landscape. Yet here I was, with a spotlight in hand, on what felt like a folklore endeavor.

"These mammals have gone from endangered, to extinct, back to endangered, to extinct, and are now making a comeback," I explained to our class, "and all because of one woman's curiosity."

I shared how after settlers arrived at the prairie in the 1800s, the black-footed ferrets began disappearing because of the "three p's": plows, poison, and plague. Black-footed ferrets' primary food source is prairie dogs. Overplowing of the land, poisoning the prairie dog "pests," and a plague introduced from distant lands led to dwindling prairie dog colonies. Ferrets couldn't find food, and when they did, they contracted the plague from their dinner.

By the 1950s, black-footed ferrets were considered extinct until a small group was discovered in 1964, only to die out fifteen years later, leading to their second extinction. That was until 1981, when a Wyoming rancher discovered the carcass of a large rodent left by his ranch dog. While the rancher wanted to toss the deceased animal into the field, his wife stopped him. She was curious about the odd-looking creature and brought it to a local taxidermist, who recognized the rodent as a black-footed ferret. They called in local wildlife biologists, who discovered 130 surviving black-footed ferrets on the ranch.

When the plague and distemper began killing off the remaining ferrets in 1984, biologists rushed in to save the remaining eighteen ferrets. This is where our nation's intensive efforts to reestablish the population began. Those eighteen ferrets became the ancestors of our current black-footed ferret population in the United States.[1]

Researching the history of these animals and the extreme efforts to protect their vulnerable lives, I couldn't help but think it was a lost cause. As the plague regularly makes its round to prairie dogs in the same way the common cold circles around to my children, ferrets die off in droves. Their third extinction looms, seemingly inevitable. It begs the question: What is our responsibility as believers in protecting creation when we understand it is "subject to futility"(Rom. 8:20)?

"There!" A gentleman fixed his spotlight on a mound of dirt sixty feet from us. "I saw a green reflection."

We all stared.

"I see it!" I whispered excitedly. The silhouette of a long figure poked up from behind the mound. I didn't get to see his flashy eyes, but I made out his form. And that's all we got. But it was sufficient. It was enough to keep me teaching these classes and educating others about the power of curiosity.

If one rancher's wife's curiosity can save an entire species, even if just for a time, then perhaps my interest can also make a difference. This is the power of caring for God's creation. Perhaps one reason he calls us to steward the earth is so that we can ignite curiosity and care in our children's hearts. As together we explore the fascinating world he has made, our children will find reason to protect it so they can carry on a contagious curiosity and point others to God through what he has made.

## A Childlike Faith

"Wonder ought never to go," the theologian Oswald Chambers once said. "With a child the element of wonder is always there, a freshness and spontaneity, and the same is true of those who follow Jesus Christ's teaching and become as little children."[2]

We often think of the faith of a child as an ingrained, intuitive faith undiluted and undefiled by our life experiences and doubt. A child is quick to trust. But that can leave us with this tension: Is this blind faith? Yet *childlike* faith is not *childish*. *Childish* is a silliness and immaturity that ideally we grow out of. *Childlike*, on the other hand, extracts the beauty and wonder from how a child views the world. It is not jaded by life's disappointments and defeats. It is not naive, but rather pure. Untarnished. Optimistic. Fresh. A childlike faith is closer to its source—more in tune with the Maker. Surrounded by the wonders of creation, you can revive your own childlike faith while simultaneously preserving it in your children.

We read in Luke 18:15–17:

> Now they were bringing even infants to him that he might touch them. And when the disciples saw it, they rebuked them. But Jesus called them to him, saying, "Let the children come to me, and do not hinder them, for to such belongs the kingdom of God. Truly, I say to you, whoever does not receive the kingdom of God like a child shall not enter it."

Why does the kingdom of God belong to children? Perhaps because their faith rests not on naivety but on wonder. They see the evidence of God in creation. They stand beneath a rainbow, before a waterfall, or beside a bird's nest, and they know God is real.

In Matthew 18:3–4, Jesus's words affirm the importance of childlike faith: "Truly, I say to you, unless you turn and become like children, you will never enter the kingdom of heaven. Whoever humbles himself like this child is the greatest in the kingdom of heaven." If we as adults forfeit curiosity, we lose a critical element of faith. We stop looking for, and eventually stop seeing, the evidence for God all around us. Further, we quit asking questions. We become vulnerable to false philosophies and ideas, and we're less equipped to help our children think critically and come to their own conclusions guided by God's Word. We must remain curious about creation and what it tells us about God.

"Whoever humbles himself," Jesus said in the above Scripture. Nature fosters this humility. I remember an overwhelming feeling of smallness when we moved to Colorado. Standing in a sprawling meadow hemmed by massive summits, you cannot help but feel dwarfed. Nature helps us remember our place in this world. In a society yelling that you must be heard, known, seen, and standing on a stage, creation reminds us what matters is not that the world sees us but that our Maker does. Perhaps that is why he sculpted the summits so high, wound the rivers so long, and stretched out the meadows wide and sprawling. Standing small in the middle of it all, we know our place. We become comfortable with smallness.

God hung each star in the sky. He arcs every rainbow across the horizon. He created all of this and called it "good." Then he created us, his children, and calls us "very good." Nature reminds us we are not the center of the world. Yet at the same time, it assures us we are God's focus. We are his favorite creation. We need these reminders often. They anchor our perspective and ground our faith.

We can watch this faith taking shape and form, bent and sculpted and chiseled by hours outside. I saw it one day as we meandered through the forest and my oldest son exclaimed, "Mom, a waterfall!"

His little brother eagerly followed, excitement setting his quick pace. "Oh! A waterfall!"

"Mom, this is our playground." My oldest scrambled atop a boulder. The boys have these certain looks and smiles, a depth in their eyes reserved for those holy moments when their spirits are overwhelmed by wonder.

As I watch them balance across the dark, twisted trunk of a fallen pine tree, or observe them scaling boulders, I see them beholding something more significant than I could ever offer. This is a beauty I could never create for them. This is a peace I could never fabricate. This is an imagination I could never inspire. This is a way of play I could never orchestrate. This is an awe I could never script. I can only bring them to where these things are found and set them down in the midst of God's glory. And the more their tiny hearts grasp this magnificence, the more they want it. They are drawn to mystery, artistry, intrigue, and delight. It awakens them. Or maybe it keeps them from falling asleep, as many of us adults have become numb to wonder. These experiences tug at their hearts and tell them this is right. This is good. This is the work of their Creator.

Witnessing these moments of awe unfurling like a flower at the height of its bloom, we realize the power of curiosity. God's glory reflected in creation beckons us to explore further. Surrounded by beauty, we rediscover the faith of a child, fueled by curiosity and rooted in wonder.

## Step Outside

God placed curiosity in your children's minds and spirits to compel them in their pursuit of him. If nature is a place where we find him, then curiosity is the compass guiding us. Your children's discovery of God does not depend entirely on your knowledge of nature or the Bible. Instead, your children's God-given curiosity will be of great help in this adventure.

If you fear your children have lost touch with their curiosity, begin spending longer periods of time outside. Explore different natural settings such as woods, beaches, swamps, ponds, rivers, and fields.

Keep exploring until a small flicker of curiosity is fanned and flamed into a passionate pursuit of their Maker.

## See Nature in the Bible

Ask your children what one of their favorite things in nature is. Share with them what one of your favorite natural things is. You can also tell them what natural things you loved as a child, and if you collected anything in nature. Explain to them that God talks about nature all throughout the Bible. Here are some collections of nature verses to explore together depending on your children's interests:

- *Birds*: Job 12:7–10; Psalm 50:11; 84:1–3; 104:12, Isaiah 40:31; Jeremiah 8:7; Luke 12:24
- *Animals*: Genesis 1:24–25; Job 12:7–10; Psalm 104:18, 24; Proverbs 12:10; Isaiah 63:13
- *Fish and sea creatures*: Genesis 1:20–21; Job 12:7–10; Psalm 69:34; 104:25; Matthew 4:18–19; 12:40
- *Trees and plants*: Genesis 1:12; Psalm 1:1–3; 104:14, 16; Ezekiel 47:12; John 15:4
- *Mountains*: Psalm 90:2; 104:8, 18; 121:1–2; Isaiah 54:10; Amos 4:13; Nahum 1:5
- *The sky*: Genesis 1:16; Psalm 8:1, 3–4; 19:1; 33:6, 104:19, 136:7–9
- *Water*: Psalm 1:3; 104:6–11, 13, 25; Isaiah 12:3; 55:10; Jeremiah 17:8; John 4:13–14
- *Seasons*: Genesis 8:22; Psalm 104:19, 27–28; Ecclesiastes 3:1; Isaiah 55:10

## See God in Nature

Take a walk in nature with your children. It can be through a field, along a river, in a green space adjacent to a park, on the beach; anywhere where nature can be found. However, the more natural objects they can explore, the better. Consider an area full of things to play with such as:

- Pinecones
- Branches
- Rocks
- Shells
- Bark
- Insects
- Leaves
- Fallen nests
- Flowers
- Grasses

Allow your children to play at their leisure, and watch what catches their attention. Do they construct a balancing rock tower? Do they watch a procession of ants carrying food to a hole? Do they build a stick fort? Do they collect rocks? Do they reroute a stream or build a dam?

See what piques their interest and fuel that curiosity. Head to the library and check out every picture book you can find on the topic. Spread out art supplies and encourage them to draw, paint, or somehow recreate what they loved playing with in nature. Research the topic and share fun facts about it together. Allow them to chase down that interest, and take the journey alongside them. As you're exploring and discovering, ask your children what we can learn about God from these gifts of nature.

— 5 —

# Becoming a Wonder Conservationist

*Fighting what many see as a losing battle*
*might seem a fool's errand if there were not*
*compelling reasons to do so.*

DOUGLAS W. TALLAMY

WHETHER OR NOT YOU HAVE heard the term *recency bias*, you have probably experienced it. Recency bias, otherwise known as the frequency illusion, happens when you learn something new and then begin seeing it everywhere. This will occur as you spend more time in nature.

If you learn the name of a plant, bird, or insect, you will likely begin noticing it around you much more. As you notice it, you'll care more about it. This is a natural path toward protecting the earth. Yet you might also feel the tension that I have: If Earth has an end date and the Bible clearly shows it will be destroyed, how much time and effort should we invest in protecting it?

As you experience God in nature, you'll settle into a solid understanding of biblical stewardship that you can pass along to your children. You will discover nature to be an incredible means of sharing God's love with your children and others. I've witnessed this in my own family while out in the woods, as well as in our back yard.

My youngest son positioned his foot on the top of a small garden trowel. He used his hand to steady himself against the backside of our house as he pressed the might of his leg down on the shovel. It nudged an inch, and he repositioned to try again.

The dirt was hard. Clay baked in time. In any other circumstance, I'd worry the soil might not be suitable to welcome roots and life. But the plants we were sowing into it require this exact soil. Each small hole took ten minutes to dig. Carefully we positioned into them unimpressive balls of roots. Firecracker penstemon, blue harebell, yellow columbine, blue spiderwort (an unfortunate name for a beautiful flower), and prairie red coneflowers overtook the small garden plot. But at the time, they looked like unremarkable clumps of grass and leaves. A few were browning from the week they'd spent in their plastic garden trays, waiting for my attention.

"The first year they sleep, the second year they creep, the third year they leap!" our printed garden guide assured us. I wondered if we'd see any blooms this year. I questioned, too, if I should trust the instructions. Water them when we plant, then let them be. It felt wrong not to keep watering, but then I looked at the prairie beside our neighborhood. Things grow there without much water. They belong here in this desert land.

We placed our final root clump and carefully spread mulch between each plant. Our Native Pollinator Garden was complete. We waited for blooms and butterflies. The first few weeks, I feared they were too dry. Stretches of days passed without rain. Then a small grouping of clouds formed and let out a misting; that was all, but it was sufficient. Timid, uncommitted rain coaxed blooms into blossoms. Blue harebell made the first appearance with their delicate bell-shaped blooms hanging from dainty stems. Red prairie coneflowers followed. "Rocket flowers," my children dubbed them when we discovered them out in the foothills. A cone points toward the sky with red and yellow petals trailing behind like fire bursting from a rocket on its next moon mission.

I was stunned by how well our garden took off, but then I felt silly for the surprise. I have witnessed these same plants thriving across our natural areas. Why would they not do just as well here, in their same native soil? The same is true for us and our children. We can thrive in difficult conditions if it's where God means for us to be. He gives us all we need to flourish no matter our circumstances.

On an early summer afternoon, I ran along a wooded path twenty minutes from home. June in Colorado is magical. The wildflowers unfurl in perfect sequence, a symphony of summer. I stopped, recognizing the long creeping stems of a blue spiderwort plant. I wouldn't have known its name except that it had bloomed in our pollinator garden a week before. I became familiar with the flowers because I had joined their mission: feed the bees and butterflies. Create stopovers and refueling centers for traveling droves of insects and birds. Try, however we may, to preserve what is quickly fading from this planet.

As a follower of Jesus, I understand this world is broken and bent on decay. As a naturalist, it pains me to watch the process. As a mom, I want my children to understand our roles and responsibility. Yes, this planet has a time stamp. The disappearance of beautiful things is inevitable. In the meantime, however, we get to preserve as much as we can for as long as we can. We get to protect and point to evidence of our Creator, drawing attention to the wonders he has made. We get to share the gospel through the myriad of visuals he's given us in creation. This is why in our garden, we dig through impossible soil. We know we are fighting a losing battle, but we have a compelling reason. If our acts of stewardship and preservation keep one gift of nature around for a little longer, maybe we can point someone to the Creator.

As your children participate in caring for living things, they connect with an eternal purpose. They carry out a God-given initiative. As a result, they learn not only about keeping things alive but also about patience, respect, generosity, selflessness, and the pursuit of true beauty.

*A Sand County Almanac* was first published in 1949. Its author, Aldo Leopold, was a man who had seen the Great Depression and was now witnessing a postwar economic boom. America was hyper-focused on defining what held value. The land was sapped of every morsel of value for agriculture. But what about the songbird? What about the plants and creatures that were of no use in economic growth? Every living thing in an ecosystem has an important role and makes the entire habitat stronger. Leopold wrote about my home state, "Of the 22,000 higher plants and animals native to Wisconsin, it is doubtful more than 5 per cent can be sold, fed, eaten, or otherwise put to economic use."[1] He stated that shortfalls, overlooks, and negligence in conservation have historically stemmed from the thought that if something natural doesn't hold economic value, it's unimportant.

But can something with no apparent fiscal advantage hold eternal value? Is a lovely thing valuable simply for its loveliness? Philippians 4:8 says, "Whatever is true, whatever is honorable, whatever is just, whatever is pure, whatever is lovely, whatever is commendable, if there is any excellence, if there is anything worthy of praise, think about these things."

In this passage, we find the virtues of "lovely" and "true" related to each other. Pairing together "lovely" and "true," we step into the domain of evidence. The loveliness of a black-capped chickadee or rock wren holds some truth. It points attention to a Creator. The value of these creatures becomes—or it should become—the believer's concern.

It is the existence of beautiful things we want to preserve as well as access to them. Going back to our example of Abram listening to God's promise beneath a brilliant spread of stars, we see that the sky itself was a catalyst for his faith. Genesis 15:5–6 says, "And he brought him outside and said, 'Look toward heaven, and number the stars, if you are able to number them.' Then he said to him, 'So shall your offspring be.' And he believed the LORD, and he counted it to him as righteousness." The sky—and the One who spoke it into place—convinced Abram.

Have you ever experienced a connection in nature that so solidified your belief in a Creator? One month before the Cameron Peak fire sparked, we spent a day exploring the wilderness areas at the top of the canyon an hour's drive from our home. Our oldest son straddled a foot on each side of a tiny creek.

"This is the headwaters for the Colorado River," my husband explained to us, "which carved the Grand Canyon."

It is not much more than a trickle. If you're not looking for it, you'll miss it. We stood and wondered a million thoughts. The water carried our ponderings hundreds of miles to where perhaps another family stood, six thousand feet high on a canyon ridge, wondering a million thoughts of their own before sending them, alongside our own, to the sea.

It is places like those, with soggy earth squishing between their toes and surrounded by wildflowers, where my children experience their Creator. As with Abram beneath the stars, creation solidifies what they innately know—there is a mighty God who loves them.

One month later, the entire area surrounding the headwaters of the Colorado River was engulfed in flames and would be closed to access for over a year. Had we been a month later, we'd have missed our opportunity to stand, awestruck, over that tiny yet powerful creek. After forest roads reopened and my family ventured back into those same woods, they were very different.

This is why I choose to enter into discussion and efforts around conservation, not because I believe we can save the planet—we cannot—but instead, because I believe God has called us to steward what he has created. In doing so, we can make this earth a better place to inhabit and enjoy until its time is over. But more importantly, we can protect the elements and areas in nature that serve as evidence of the Creator. These are the materials God can and will use to convince our children of his existence and love.

## Biblical Stewardship

What do you think of when you hear the word *stewardship*? To steward something well is to take care of and protect it. If you have stewarded something—or in the case of parenting, someone—why did you do it?

God's idea of stewardship extends far beyond a management role. When he gives us something or someone to take care of, we feel a deep sense of personal responsibility. We understand we have been entrusted with something extraordinary. Biblical stewardship is a sacred act of caring for that which God has given us. Further, it compels us to take action that we believe has eternal dividends. When we care for and protect nature, we discover, within what is temporary and decaying, eternal elements. We can use everything God created to point our kids to his glory and wisdom.

"When the caterpillar bites the stem vein, the leaf falls over like that," I explained to my children as we walked through a nature preserve in Denver. We perched on a downed pine tree, observing a patch of milkweed plants below. It was too late in the year for flowers, but limp leaves provided the subject of our lesson.

"Insects don't eat this plant because the sap is too sticky. When they bite into it, it glues their mouths shut. But the monarch caterpillar learned that if it chews through the leaf vein, it stops the flow of sap from getting to the leaf. Then they can eat."

The monarch's method of survival nearly led to its extinction. As a "specialized species," they depend solely on milkweed. All their eggs are in one basket, or, quite literally, on one plant species. Intensive efforts have been made to plant milkweed "corridors" for the monarch butterflies. Because of these efforts, their population has been restored to hopeful levels.

I stared at the limp leaf and considered what it teaches about toxicity in our lives. What if we, too, learned to identify toxic thoughts and habits and cut them off at their source? Had the monarchs disappeared, we wouldn't have this visual. I made a mental note to add milkweed to our garden.

When we grow, nurture, and protect creation, we enter into God's work. In the first garden, God placed work ethic into the human heart. Work was not a symptom of the fall, but a gift given before sin entered the garden gates. In Genesis 2:15, we see humankind's first assignment: "The LORD God took the man and put him in the garden of Eden to work it and keep it." God called forth a garden, placed Adam in the middle, and planted purpose in his soul.

Have you ever felt that pulse of purpose as you've dug fingers into damp soil or plucked a ripe tomato straight from the vine? God created us to cultivate and nurture life, yet our experience is only a ripple of what Adam must have partaken in. Adam landed the most magnificent horticultural job of all time! He assumed ownership and tended to this brilliant, perfect utopian garden. It was the only garden in all of Earth's history bent on flourishing without any handicap. Every bud bloomed to its fullest potential. Each fruit ripened to its most succulent form. Can you imagine the fragrance, colors, textures, and tastes? There was so much in that garden that has since gone extinct. Oh, to be a fly on the Tree of Life, taking it all in!

What an honor it would have been to cultivate such a garden. We can only imagine the simplicity of life at that time. With no society to manage or need for government, land stewardship was the only job. It was the foundation of history and humanity. Genesis offers us a brief synopsis of land stewardship and its progression. It begins in Genesis 2 with Adam as a gardener. Soon after, in Genesis 4:2, we see Abel keeping sheep and Cain raising crops. In chapter 9, we find Noah dressing vines. Isaac, in Genesis 26:12, is farming the land.

When God wrote the job description for land stewardship, he gave Adam an incredible gift packed with significance and purpose, one with guaranteed success . . . until everything broke. A chapter after he landed the job, pride disqualified him. Adam and Eve invited sin into the garden. We read God's words to Adam in Genesis 3:17–18: "Because you have listened to the voice of your wife and have eaten of the tree of which I commanded you, 'You shall not eat of it,' cursed is the ground because of you; in pain you shall eat of it all the days of your life; thorns and thistles it shall bring forth for you; and you shall eat the plants of the field."

Do you imagine Adam knew, at that moment, a tiny fraction of the effects of his decision? He and Eve had set off a chain reaction, and they couldn't have predicted even half the repercussions. Perhaps in God's description of "thorns and thistles," he could envision weeds taking over and choking life from the garden. But could he foresee what this curse would introduce? Pestilence. Drought. Famine. Extinction. Flooding. Disease. He and his wife had, in one moment, set off and disrupted the planet's balance for all time. They had introduced each challenge, heartache, impossibility, and devastation every farmer, agriculturist, and ecologist struggles against.

Narrowing our focus to Isaac's farm, we're offered a glimpse of hope. Genesis 26:12 says, "And Isaac sowed in that land and reaped in the same year a hundredfold. The LORD blessed him." *Blessing from the cursed ground.* The God who bends nature's laws and works into those laws scenarios we're apt to label as miracles can bring fruit from parched places. He is bigger than the curse. As a result, we can hold to the significance and purpose of land stewardship without succumbing to the discouragement of Earth's futility.

Conservation is not a lost cause; it is a limited cause. Understanding that stewarding the creation God has given us is a mission with an end date, we can work faithfully while there is still time. God's Word is packed with promises around that faithful work:

> Therefore, my beloved brothers and sisters, be firm, immovable, always excelling in the work of the Lord, knowing that your labor is not in vain in the Lord. (1 Cor. 15:58 NASB)

> I planted, Apollos watered, but God gave the growth. So neither he who plants nor he who waters is anything, but only God who gives the growth. (1 Cor. 3:6–7)

> And let us not grow weary of doing good, for in due season we will reap, if we do not give up. (Gal. 6:9)

> Let the favor of the Lord our God be upon us, and establish the work of our hands upon us; yes, establish the work of our hands! (Ps. 90:17)

> I am the vine; you are the branches. Whoever abides in me and I in him, he it is that bears much fruit, for apart from me you can do nothing. (John 15:5)

We often read these verses in the broader context of work and faithfulness. What if we fine-tuned our focus to the work of conserving evidence of a Creator and preserving wonder and curiosity for the next generation?

Perhaps the extinction we should be even more concerned with is the extinction of wonder, curiosity, and care. Even more quickly than the earth's resources are being depleted, we're losing interest in what is still available. We could call this new endeavor *Wonder*

*Conservation.* As we preserve the God-given sense of wonder in children, their interest evolves into stewardship. They develop an intense appreciation of and care for nature. Perhaps it begins with the same first assignment given to Adam: naming nature.

## Naming Nature

Think of a specific bird. What came to mind first? Do you have a story or special connection to that species that pulled it into your memory? Think now about a place in nature. What is its name? When we have special nature experiences, we tend to remember names and specifics about that thing or place. We become familiar with it. I've watched this happen with my children as they have become (and encouraged me to become) avid bird-watchers.

"An oriole!" my second son—my normally *quiet* son—exclaimed loudly from the back seat of our SUV.

My gaze darted from branch to branch along the cottonwoods hugging the lakeshore.

The fiery orange wings of a migrating Bullock's oriole caught my attention. The contrast against the spring green leaves was remarkable.

This was our first stop of the day, a day marked on the calendar with the specific purpose of finding birds. It was the first annual Colorado Birding Challenge. Birders from across the state were competing to count as many species as possible in a twenty-four-hour window.

My sons comprised one of the three registered youth teams. The "Dangerous Ducks," as they'd dubbed their team, had worked for weeks leading up to the event, learning new species, creating flyers, and gathering sponsors for their team. They had raised over one hundred dollars that would go toward conservation efforts for migrating bird species.

I had counted on this first stop to be a promising start to the day.

Every year we find migrating birds here. The path winds between a lake to the west and the river to the east. We find riparian, wetland, river, and lake birds. After spotting only a couple of birds, we had nearly given up. Minutes ago, we'd packed up the car to head to another destination.

At my son's exclamation, we all piled back out of the car. We stayed for another hour identifying several more migrating species and resident species that call this area home year-round.

Naturalist and author Kenn Kaufman wrote in his book *A Season on the Wind*, "The woods are alive with birds—but at a glance, you might not notice them at all. Your eyes need time to adjust."[2]

Once our eyes adjusted, we began seeing them everywhere. Yellow-rumped warblers—a plump, round songbird with vivid blue markings—traveled in small groups from tree to tree. Yellow warblers sang from branches. We found more Bullock's orioles along with their uniquely engineered hanging nests.

"Did you guys find something?" I asked a pair of bicyclists who had stopped along the path and stood scanning tree trunks with their binoculars.

"There are a group of yellow warblers in that tree," they responded with eager enthusiasm.

I stood beside them, staring at the cottonwood. Our crew of young ornithologists—all three of our boys, their little sister, and a neighbor buddy who joined us for our morning—meandered the path with binoculars and our bird identification book.

"Are you all a part of the birding event?" one of the gentlemen asked me.

I was surprised he knew what we were doing. "Yes! Our boys are a team in the youth division."

The gentleman introduced himself as the event coordinator. Of all the counties participating and all the natural areas across our one county, we were birding in the same location. I have an intense gratitude for individuals like him, giving their time to conserving wonder. Because of their efforts, my kids spent an entire day outside staring at trees, water, and sky.

Over twelve hours and 197 miles, we identified forty-one species. My boys took third place of three youth teams, but they were not discouraged or deterred. Instead, they were proud of the new personal record they set and determined to find even more species the following year.

Our adventures in identifying birds have also led to identifying mammals, insects, flowers, and other plants. It has required little more than library books, a pair of binoculars, and copious amounts of time outside. As Ken Kauffman wrote, it requires enough time for our eyes to adjust.

This adjustment takes less time the more we go outside. We become acutely aware of our surroundings and quicker to notice what—or who—is around us.

In a scene in the classic children's book *Heidi*, young Heidi becomes enamored with the mountain summits surrounding her grandfather's home.

"Why do the mountains have no names, Grandfather?" Heidi asks.

"They all have names," he assures her, "and if you tell me their shape, I can name them for you."[3]

Often, it's the intricate details and beauty of something that lead us to its name. And it is those details that engrave its name into our memories.

Most of the time, it won't take you much effort to encourage your children's pursuits in nature. Many times, they only need a simple nudge or a little bit of direction. The most significant impact we can make is surrounding them by natural wonders. This can be done through books, magazines, documentaries, museums, nature centers, and classes—all complemented by time outdoors. As you provide your children a buffet of natural curiosities, they will gravitate toward specific subjects. While my oldest son loves birds, my middle son enjoys fossils and rocks. Insects are a great place to start with kindergartners, as they're plentiful and many kids around that age are eager to observe bugs. As you pay attention to your children's unique interests, you can equip them with identification guides full of colorful illustrations, then set them loose and let their curiosity lead them forward.

The saying "It takes a village to raise a child" can be true of nature exploration as well. We're not in this alone. Other adults can affirm and encourage our kids' outdoor interests. Older generations feel a surge of hope seeing kids playing outside. Nostalgia drips into our souls like a life-giving IV when we watch kids building forts, making mud pies, and chasing butterflies.

A few months after participating in the Colorado Birding Challenge, I received an email from the same organization inviting grant applications for youth education opportunities. The organization was looking to provide grant money to kids wanting to learn about birding. I'd previously learned about a three-day birding course and excursion in the Rocky Mountains that I wanted to attend with my son, but the registration cost for both of us along with lodging was outside our budget.

My son set to work writing an application, which included an essay about the opportunity, what he hoped to learn from the course, and how he would use new knowledge to educate others on bird conservation. His grant was approved, and he and I spent four days learning from master ornithologists, banding birds with their identification tags, and hiking through the Rocky Mountains, learning to identify species. We had an unforgettable bonding experience in nature because a group of adults decided to invest in my son's birding interests.

The chances are that you know adults who have special interests and expertise in nature. Who do you know has a biology degree, loves bird-watching, or raises reptiles? Do you know someone who is familiar with local area hikes, or who can name wildflowers or trees in your local park? I recently had the opportunity to be that person for someone else's child.

After I led a kids' birding walk for our natural areas department, one mom wrote in the after-class survey about her own love for bird-watching and wanting her son to develop an interest in birds. She shared her desire for him to spend less time with a screen and more time outdoors and that the experience inspired him to be outside finding birds. People who love nature love to share their passion with others. Find those people, whether they are in your circle of acquaintances, guides for your local natural areas, or volunteers with the city, and ask them to take you and your children on a walk.

## Foraging for Familiarity

Learning to name something in nature is one thing; discovering what is edible takes our familiarity with the land a level deeper.

"Watch." My husband pointed our youngest son's attention to birds on the branches above us. "They're eating chokeberries just like we did."

We were three miles into an out-and-back hike. Three of our kids were climbing trees. Grayson and I sat side by side watching robins gorge on deep violet chokeberries. One gathered a crop full then flit to an overhanging cottonwood branch. His orange belly blended with the tree's yellowing late-September leaves. One by one, he spit out pits from the tiny berries, much like my kids spit pits from cherries throughout the summer.

Back on the path, I was distracted by a grouping of sumac bushes. Their lemonade berries looked less than appetizing: shriveled, tacky, and with tiny white hairs. I filled an empty water bottle to make lemonade tea at home. I popped sticky berry clusters into the bottle as Grayson and the kids ran ahead to the next water crossing.

"What are you finding?" A group of four adults stopped, curious about my foraging.

I directed their attention to the dry ground. Vines webbed between the sumac bushes. "I've never picked these before, but you can make tea from them. And these down below are ground cherries."

"That's what the kids back there mentioned to us!" one of the hikers exclaimed.

"Oh yes, they're mine." I smiled, motioning to my kids up ahead on the trail.

"Smart kids," the gentleman beside her remarked.

I thanked him and plucked a fruit from the vine below. Ground cherries are wrapped in delicate paper packaging, resembling a Chinese lantern or tomatillo. I peeled back the wrapping to reveal a plump berry inside. Its flavor is a meld of acidic tomato with sweet pineapple. On a late September day such as this was, they're warmed from the sun, as if baked inside their paper, and absolutely delicious.

"Here, try one." I held it out to one of the ladies.

Bravely she took it and popped it into her mouth.

If I hadn't had my edible plant book, I would never risk handing a stranger fare from the woods, but I was confident in the identification. Besides, we feasted on them an hour before and were still standing.

"Oh wow," she said, turning to her hiking partners, "that's good."

"There are more over here." I pointed to a small patch along the path. "Enjoy!" I left them to their foraging.

For too long, I cautioned my kids against eating any berries in the woods. Passing by an ominous red berry or a sumac bush which can often be poisonous, I'd tell them to leave it be. Now, with our edible plant book as a companion, the woods have become friendlier.

Earlier on the path, we had passed up peavine after identifying it as poisonous, but besides that, we found five edible plant varieties.

"You don't have to like it all, but you do need to try it," my husband explained to our children. The chokeberries have a bitter aftertaste and leave your mouth dry. The robins don't seem to mind, but I stopped snacking after a few.

"Foraging is for survival," he went on. "If you ever find yourselves unprepared, you'll know what you can eat. Plus, your friends will think it's cool if you can pluck something from the tree and eat it!"

At the end of our hike, we knew the path intimately. It was welcoming, providing, promising, and fruitful. We knew its bushes and trees, and we took part with the birds. We understood more fully the provision spoken of in Genesis 1:29: "And God said, 'Behold, I have given you every plant yielding seed that is on the face of all the earth, and every tree with seed in its fruit. You shall have them for food.'"

Connected in a new way to our landscape, we're more likely to fight for it, preserve it, and share discoveries with those around us. The more we come to know a place, the more we care for it. Our actions bend toward protecting that which we care for. Perhaps it's why, back in the garden of Eden, the first task God gave Adam was to name the creatures. Knowing their names and connecting with their identities, he would be a better caretaker. What if we all pursued this Edenic familiarity with the land around us? Maybe it will change how we view preservation, and perhaps it will help us all become better Wonder Conservationists.

## Step Outside

Your children are created in God's image, and they share his compassionate heart. He has wired them to care about the things he has made. Depending on their age and experiences, it might be difficult to see a stewardship spirit within them, but it can be revived. The most effective way to encourage your children in caring for creation is to help them become familiar with God's art. Pay close attention to what they gravitate toward. Whatever they show a special interest in, help them explore it further. Check out books, visit a museum, take a class, watch a documentary, and ask experts on that topic to guide you and your children on a walk or hike.

As your children become more interested, look for a way to help them become actively involved. If they're interested in birds, build a birdhouse or install birdfeeders in your yard. If they like flowers or insects, plant a small garden with native plants that help pollinators. If they like turtles, spend a morning picking up trash by a local pond. Provide them opportunities to practice compassion and care for creation. As they practice biblical stewardship, they'll become Wonder Conservationists helping others experience the joy and purpose in protecting God's world.

### See Nature in the Bible

- Help your children explore the many ways God calls his children to care for his creation. You can pair these biblical examples with trips or documentaries about those pursuing these specific calls to stewardship:
  » Read Genesis 2:15, and take your children to visit a local garden or talk to a gardener about the work they do and why they do it.
  » Read Genesis 4:2, and visit a local sheep farm or check out library books on keeping sheep. You can talk about how shepherds protect their sheep, and God is our shepherd protecting us. You can also read them Psalm 23 and talk about the specific ways God comforts and protects us.
  » Read Genesis 9:20 in the ESV translation. Point out that "Noah began to be a man of the soil." Ask your children what

they think that means, and how we can be "people of the soil" helping to grow and protect God's creation.

» Read Genesis 26:12–14 and discuss how God blessed the land and Isaac. Share how God helped Isaac become wealthy not only with money but in experiences. We are wealthy with joy and purpose when we join God's work of growing good things.

• Ask your children what they think would happen if people stopped caring about nature or growing and protecting what God has made.

## See God in Nature

A conservationist not only protects natural things, but they also inspire others to get involved! Be a Wonder Conservationist by inspiring others to plant with you. Throw a "Planting Party" where a handful of friends can discover the life-giving practice of preserving nature. It doesn't need to (and shouldn't) be elaborate or complicated. Simply set out some popcorn and fruit to munch on. Provide seeds, soil, and containers, and encourage others to take part in God's act of making all things new! Here are a few ideas to run with:

• Plant baby trees outside.
• Plant potted vegetables.
• Sow flower seeds into pots.
• Plant milkweed for monarchs, and read a picture book from the library about monarch butterfly migration.
• Plant grass seed in pots for quick-growing foliage.
• Repot or "propagate" succulents.
• Create indoor ecosystems with terrariums. Download my free Terrarium Planting Activity + Bible Lesson at www.erynlynum .com/terrarium.

— 6 —

# The Absolute Truth About Nature

*The solid world exists, its laws do not change.*
*Stones are hard, water is wet.*
GEORGE ORWELL

WATCHING YOUR CHILDREN'S IMAGINATION DEVELOP is a remarkable experience. Yet in today's society, kids are facing a dilemma of imagination that results in a skewed perception of reality. "Imagine whatever you want," the world tells your children, "and that can be *your truth.*"

All around, our kids hear that *their reality* is what's right for them, and *someone else's reality* is what is right for that individual. Popular thought says everything is fluid and flexible to our own interpretations. But our God is a God of order and peace. He never meant for our kids' magnificent imaginations to lead them into confusion or chaos, which is what these false ideas do. By showing our kids the indisputable characteristics of nature, we can show them that there is one reality rooted in the truth of God's Word and evident throughout his designs.

You don't have to let society funnel your children's imagination into its false agendas. Instead, you can recapture your children's wonder and recenter it on our good and creative God. Our kids can discover God's life-giving methods, as my sons realized one day through a simple game.

We stood in a parking garage preparing for a walk around the lake. My sons entertained themselves with made-up games while they waited for us. They stood at the bottom of a concrete staircase, preparing to climb the flight, then race back down.

My oldest son stated emphatically to his two younger brothers, "The only rule is, there are no rules."

"Hold on a second," I told them, strapping their little sister into her stroller. "So if someone wants to jump off the top of the parking garage to the concrete below, they can?"

"No," my son responded, his answer hung in the air, waiting to hook onto a resolution. "Ok," he relented, "the only rule is you cannot jump off."

I challenged him further. "If they want to roll down the concrete stairs, is that ok?"

"No, not that either, you cannot roll down the stairs." He was growing irritated.

"So," I concluded, "not having rules doesn't really work, does it?"

He agreed then ran up the stairs for a head start in front of his brothers.

This "no rules" philosophy is a puzzle today's kids face. Have you felt a growing concern over what popular media, politics, and even curriculums are telling your children? Our kids are growing up in a world of gray space lacking definitive lines. "There are no absolutes," they're told. "Everything is up to your interpretation," and "You get to make the rules."

In his book *Mere Christianity*, C. S. Lewis shares what he saw as an obvious disconnect in this popular worldview. It was a paradox that ultimately led him to Jesus. He wrote:

My argument against God was that the universe seemed so cruel and unjust. But how had I got this idea of *just* and *unjust*? A man does not call a line crooked unless he has some idea of a straight line. What was I comparing this universe with when I called it unjust? . . . Thus in the very act of trying to prove that God did not exist—in other words, that the whole of reality was senseless—I found I was forced to assume that one part of reality—namely my idea of justice—was full of sense. Consequently atheism turns out to be too simple. If the whole universe has no meaning, we should never have found out that it has no meaning.[1]

In children's innocent ways—how they often perceive inconsistencies faster than adults do—I think they may know the world cannot operate without guidelines and definition. They sense the disarray and chaos resulting from everyone making up their own rules or deciding that there are none. To test this, you can take out a board game and set it in front of your children. Remove all the pieces, and arrange them in a random fashion. Throw away the rulebook. Explain to your children that you are all playing the game together, but everyone gets to make up their own rules and decide for themselves what "winning" looks like, or the goal of the game. It might be fun for a few minutes as everyone laughs at silly rules. However, as everyone bends rules in their own favor to win, and strategies tangle up and prevent anyone from forward progress, they'll realize the disarray and frustration of free-for-all play, and that it's really not all that fun.

This arena of flexible, relative rules quickly leads to the discussion of dissolvable truth, or rather, that there is no truth. The concept of truth has been made flimsy and elastic; stretching to fit whatever one desires, constricting to deny anything they don't like. This is the postmodern era our kids are spending their childhoods in. In her book *Mama Bear Apologetics*, Hillary Morgan Ferrer explains,

"The basic definition of truth is 'that which corresponds to reality.' In other words, truth is telling it like it is."[2]

Nature provides excellent, irrefutable models of absolutes. In it, we find myriad examples to show our kids God's consistent and reliable characteristics. As I was training to certify as a master naturalist, I was more convinced than ever that we do not get to slap our own definitions on nature. I can communicate natural things in a million fitting words, but I don't get to define them. The Creator already has. As your kids spend time outside, what they discover amid all the beauty is this: Nature is absolute. It is definitive. They do not get to decide whether a rock is hard or water is wet. They don't get to declare the height of a mountain or the length of a valley. It is already fixed. "He established the earth upon its foundations," we read in Psalm 104:5, 8 (NASB), "so that it will not totter forever and ever. . . . The mountains rose; the valleys sank down to the place which You established for them."

Isaiah 40:12–14 (NASB) states plainly that the world and everything in it are carefully measured by God and designed with mathematical precision:

> Who has measured the waters in the hollow of His hand,
> And measured the heavens with a span,
> And calculated the dust of the earth with a measure,
> And weighed the mountains in a balance
> And the hills in a pair of scales?
> Who has directed the Spirit of the LORD,
> Or as His counselor has informed Him?
> With whom did He consult and who gave Him
> understanding?
> And who taught Him in the path of justice and taught Him
> knowledge,
> And informed Him of the way of understanding?

There was no planning committee for the universe; only God as the trinity of Father, Son, and Spirit, who stands outside time and measurement, making all the calls. We cannot argue with nature. We have seen that in rare occurrences, God exercised his right as the lawmaker to bend or suspend nature's laws. But we as humans do not hold that power. We can mess with his designs and contaminate what he meant for good, but we do not get to redefine it. Nature presents us with unyielding rules and laws.

As C. S. Lewis put it, "a man does not call a line crooked unless he has some idea of a straight line."[3] And as our kids acquaint themselves with natural things, they can begin to recognize and identify what is artificial or contrary to God's designs. This education isn't only for our kids. The more time we as adults spend in nature, we can recognize God's intentionality and translate it to our parenting. In an ever-shifting world that we fear will sweep our children up with its false ideas, we can find stability in God's methods and means throughout creation. Time in nature clears confusion and recenters us on God's thoughts.

## Training Our Kids in Truthful Habits
Observing the absolutes of nature, our kids reconnect the dots from creation to Creator. Then, they take it one step further, tracing this concept back to their own makeup. If God so finely tuned nature, he has also designed life-giving boundaries for our lives. He has a plan and purpose. As our kids learn to see and state a thing as it is, black-and-white lines form in their minds. Boundary lines act as guardrails and map markers, leading to the abundant life God has for us, just as he designed nature to flourish. John 8:36 says, "So if the Son sets you free, you will be free indeed." God's ways liberate us from confusion and bring clarity, peace, and joy.

In the *Handbook of Nature Study*, a renowned 1939 educational publication, we read, "Nature-study aids both in discernment and in expression of things as they are."[4]

The late educator Charlotte Mason took this concept and turned it into a scene of outdoor play. She wrote of children spending time in nature: "This is all play to children, but the mother is doing invaluable work; she is training their powers of observation and expression . . . when they ask, 'What is it?' and 'What is it for?' . . . she is training her children in truthful habits, by making them careful to see the fact and to state it exactly, without omission or exaggeration."[5]

Our society exhibits a lot of omission and exaggeration, doesn't it? In a world of wishy-washy standards and blurred definitions, you can help your children practice seeing and stating a thing not as they wish it to be but as it is. This is how they grow muscles of discernment, gathering facts instead of opinions and coming to a conclusion supported by evidence.

When this exercise of acute observation has been applied to science, we find the concept of "fine-tuning." For centuries, scientists have discovered a universe meticulously designed to support life on Earth, and for that life—us as humans—to have the intellectual capacity to understand the sciences points to a Creator with an intelligent mind. In *Science and the Mind of the Maker*, Melissa Cain Travis shares the scientific and philosophical discoveries of past generations, writing, "Copernicus, Kepler, Galileo, Newton, and Boyle were key players in the scientific revolution, and all five of them saw the attributes of the cosmos as indicators of a wise Creator in whose image we are made."[6] She also notes, "Features of the universe and our planetary home appear to be customized for the existence of intelligent creatures *and* scientific activity; it is as if we were *meant* to uncover the secrets of the world around us."[7]

What if our children were to follow in the footsteps of these great scientists and philosophers? As your children explore all that has been made and practice explaining it in detail, they can discover how it points to an intelligent Creator.

Taking the lead from Charlotte Mason, I have practiced this acute observation with my children. When they come to me with a fuzzy explanation of a thing, I instruct them to go back and gather more details. "Bring those details to me," I tell them. "Then I will go and see what you are excited about."

I give them resources full of contours and crevices, nature books abounding with explanations in words and pictures. But most importantly, I let them enjoy unconfined time in nature, exploring at their leisure and spending however much time they need in front of a beautiful thing. As they do, I pray and trust they will "uncover the secrets of the world around us" and state those truths absolutely, without omission or exaggeration.

Your children can develop their observation skills through a fun guessing game with a few friends. In a natural setting, they can explain something to one another and have three guesses as to what it is. Expand the game and your child's familiarity with nature by learning the exact names for what they are describing. When they give a good description, and after you've guessed "flower," "bird," or "beetle," go with them to inspect it and find its name. Use local nature reference books from the library or an app (iNaturalist is a great one) to identify what it is. Next time, instead of guessing "a flower," children can narrow it down to "a bluebell." Instead of simply "a bird on a branch," they can guess "a finch on a spruce tree." Encourage them to always use new words to describe what they see, becoming as accurate as they can in their descriptions. As they begin noticing the intricate and defining details of nature, they'll perceive how carefully God designed everything around them.

## The Contrast of Nature

Can you recall learning about contrasting colors in art class? Contrasting colors, also known as *complementary colors*, are colors opposite of each other on the color wheel. When painting, many artists pair together contrasting colors. These opposite colors draw our attention because we appreciate contrast. It makes sense to us because at our core, we want to understand the difference between things. It is the opposite of confusing and blurry—it is *beautiful*, as my son discovered one day surrounded by winged creatures.

On a drizzly April morning, we made our way south to Denver. The kids were antsy in their seats, excited for a long-anticipated field trip. The Butterfly Pavilion felt like a perfect tropical getaway after a long winter. I quickly lost sight of the boys; they scattered this way and that on the trails, led by vibrant butterflies. I walk-ran after our three-year-old daughter as she explored paved paths winding through tropical plants dressed in massive neon flowers. Everywhere there were butterflies.

I caught up with my oldest son, and my eyes narrowed to where his had landed. It was not a brightly colored butterfly that demanded his attention. Instead, it was a humble black-and-white paper kite butterfly. While my preschool daughter chased bright colors flitting in the path before her, my son, at nearly ten years old, was drawn to something different: contrast.

The crisp lines of the paper kite butterfly's wings communicate definition. Confidence. Differentiation. Clarity. There is no gray space, no guessing, no colors bleeding into the next, no maybe, and no relativity. It is black and white. Its elegance will not allow wishy-washy conversation. From its golden chrysalis to its pearl wings dashed in onyx, the paper kite butterfly reminds us there is a Creator who spoke every species into the sky, and that Creator does not hem and haw in indecision. He is not vague about what is helpful and what is harmful. He does not bend to opinion. He is steadfast, secure, immovable, and set on truth, goodness, and all that is lovely and pure. There is no room for interpretation, only for discovering what is clearly defined. Observing nature's details, our kids can realize that God gives contrast for a reason: to help us determine what is true.

## There Is No "You Do You" in the Wilderness

As our kids learn to differentiate animal tracks, identify butterflies and flowers, and choose sturdy logs and rocks for river crossings, they subconsciously recognize the absolute qualities of nature. We might not exactly know where a coyote's tracks took him, but we don't get to change the trajectory, either. We don't define what is soft, hard, wet, or squishy. It simply is what it is. We cannot alter the bird's song because we want it to sound differently. We cannot shift the weather to better fit our agenda. A difficult mountain pass might be beyond our current capabilities, or a storm might turn us around. We don't get to make up the rules or control the outcome in the wilderness. Instead, we have to collaborate with nature's laws and its lawmaker.

"You do you" out in the wilderness can get you in a whole lot of trouble.

Take, for example, the day a moose nearly ran over my three sons. My daughter and I explored a stream nearby as my husband walked ahead with our boys along the path to Sprague Lake in Rocky Mountain National Park. They had only tossed a few casts of their fishing lines into the lake when a moose calf, around nine months old, erupted from the woods and ran directly toward them. The young moose ran straight between my husband and three boys.

Immediately Grayson scanned the forest. This calf was young, and no doubt its mama was nearby. Sure enough, after a moment, he heard the angry huffing of an enormous mammal. With the curious calf now a safe distance away, Grayson gathered the boys, and together they backed away from the trajectory of mama moose.

This is when my daughter and I casually entered the wild scene. We rounded the corner to see our men backed against a willow tree and mama moose, her ears still angrily pinned back, ushering her calf through the water to a safer shore of the lake.

This was one of a handful of close encounters we have had with moose since moving to the mountains, including an evening when out on a run, I encountered a mama moose with three calves. The giant animal is highly aggressive, especially a mama with her young. That day at the lake could have turned out differently. Had the baby moose kept close to my crew, mama could have charged. We don't get to decide the temperament of a moose. Their behavior stands outside our control. We don't get to project kindness on the moose or pretend it is anything it is not. Encounters in the wilderness teach our kids that they must wisely prepare and cooperate with nature.

## Preparing Our Kids to Navigate a Rapidly Changing World

Becoming familiar with nature's details will guide you and your children in developing habits of discernment. Just as my family, equipped with our foraging book, learned to identify and avoid dangerous plants, your children can flex their critical thinking skills and begin asking important questions about what is harmful and what is safe and beneficial.

In *Awakening Wonder*, author Sally Clarkson writes, "A child fashioned by a wonder-filled life will cultivate inner strength, a confidence in his own ability to think, evaluate, and know."[8]

Time in nature gives our kids confidence amid changing conditions. In her book *The World Is Our Classroom*, Cindy Ross shares how she and her husband took their two very young children on long-distance backcountry hiking trips stretching hundreds and even thousands of miles long. Having watched her children learn and adapt to their surroundings, Ross notes: "Knowing how to negotiate a mountain pass and how to ford a stream are worthwhile skills . . . the experience was teaching them creative problem solving. By practicing this way of thinking, they would be better equipped to navigate a rapidly changing world."[9] She goes on to explain, "Through play, kids learn that they can solve problems for themselves. They

gain confidence in their ability to negotiate life on their own. They develop coping skills and the ability to problem solve."[10]

Like the day my boys watched their daddy usher them safely out of the path of a mama moose, I want them to observe and practice how to identify and respond to threats, whether it be an aggressive animal or a false idea. This applies not only to the shifting winds or a storm front along a mountain path but also to the ever-changing circumstances in our kids' lives and the society around them.

These false ideas are bombarding our children, spreading through books, magazines, movies, and social media at an alarming pace. We cannot shield them from every wayward idea, so we must equip them to identify falsehood and combat it with truth. First Peter 5:8 says, "Be sober-minded; be watchful. Your adversary the devil prowls around like a roaring lion, seeking someone to devour."

Never did I understand this verse more clearly than when a mountain lion stood on our street yelling his deep, throaty cat call. We had spent the evening with friends around a bonfire in our back yard. Our combined eight children played freeze tag with flashlights and munched on s'mores beneath the stars.

At the end of the evening as our friends were loading up their minivan, they turned to my husband in the driveway and asked, "What is that sound?"

Grayson paused to listen, then with eyes wide responded, "A mountain lion!" He quickly called me out to the driveway so I too could hear the lion. We estimated it to be about a block away.

Living in the WUI (Wildland Urban Interface), where city meets wilderness, we're aware lions are here and take precautions, but we had never had so close an encounter. Not that he would dare come anywhere near the noise of our children playing freeze tag, but I wondered if that evening he'd been prowling around our neighborhood.

After hearing him yelling, we sent our kids back inside, but I returned to the driveway. I wanted to listen. Sometimes it's the same with the "prowling lion" our enemy. We hear his voice, and despite the threat, we're just a bit curious about what he has to say and we stick around.

Ephesians 4:14–15 warns against this entertainment of false ideas. It says that we should no longer be "tossed to and fro by the waves and carried about by every wind of doctrine, by human cunning, by craftiness in deceitful schemes. Rather, speaking the truth in love, we are to grow up in every way into him who is the head, into Christ."

Living in lion country, we've learned that our best defense is knowledge and awareness. My husband recognized the lion's call that night because he had recently spent extensive time researching how to recognize lion calls and signs. We're learning to understand how lions behave, how to know when they are around, and what to do should we ever encounter one. The same is true of the devil and his threats of false messages and agendas. As we recognize his schemes and strategies, we're better equipped to defend our families.

Nature helps our kids develop a faith that is logical and makes sense. First Peter 1:13 (NASB) instructs, "Prepare your minds for action." Will our kids be prepared when they encounter arguments against what they believe? When friends at school tell them, "That may be your truth, but my truth is different," or when the media presents a world void of truth or absolutes, will they stand firm on a foundation of sound evidence for their Creator and worldview?

This is an intellectual faith, a life lived loving God as Matthew 22:37 says, "You shall love the Lord your God with all your heart and with all your soul and with all your *mind*" (emphasis added). As parents and caregivers, we don't need to be trained in apologetics or science. We only need to take our kids outside, encourage them in careful observation and accurate descriptions of what they see, hear, taste, and smell, and draw those observations back to God.

Everything points back to and teaches us something about the One who made it. The rising sun shows us a God who splits open darkness and casts light into our spirits. The river's banks show us a God who carves out life-giving boundaries, funneling living water to our minds and souls. A field of sunflowers rising, turning, and bending to follow the sun's course throughout the day points to a Creator who made us to seek out and follow his light. In a bird's song and the design of its dual vocal cords creating two sounds simultaneously, we can consider a God who has created us to sing praise to him. In spring buds bursting from tree branches or shoots pressing through hard winter soil, we see a God who created us to thrive after difficult seasons. These visuals and materials in nature show us a God of reason and rationality, they assure us he is a God of order. Seeing these consistencies, our children learn to identify inconsistencies in society around them.

Oswald Chambers once wrote, "God intends our attention to be arrested, He does not arrest it for us."[11] We have to train our attention to what seems at first glance ordinary and mundane. His glory and splendor are more than enough to capture and captivate, but if we are not looking for it or if we hurriedly shuffle on by, we'll miss it. We must train ourselves and our children in the difficult work of being quiet, sitting still, observing, listening, and watching, but not for too long. A child isn't meant to sit still long, only *long enough*.

As we do this, albeit imperfectly and at times clumsily, we can trust God's Holy Spirit to be at work in the souls of our kids. Psalm 25:15 says, "My eyes are ever toward the LORD." Time in nature is an active practice of continually turning our attention to God. He created our kids and us to know him through what he has made. As we give our kids the opportunity to meet him in nature, he won't allow those experiences to return void. He'll meet our kids outside and show them the reality of his love.

## Step Outside

God has given us resources in nature to equip our kids against the enemy's schemes. As your children explore, study, and appreciate nature's details, their faith will gain substance that society's false ideas cannot puncture. While today's modern ideas try to convince your children they get to decide what their personal reality and truth is, nature has a different message—one that makes a lot more sense. The more time we spend with our kids outside, the more clearly they perceive the truth behind all God has made. They learn there are definite rules and laws in nature that, if we try to change, we can get in a lot of trouble or danger. When we live, work, and play in cooperation with nature's laws, we have a safer and more enjoyable time. In this interactive education, our kids discover that God sets life-giving boundaries, and that those rules are for our good. Living in his truth, we discover the reality of his goodness and power.

### See Nature in the Bible

- Take your children to a body of water such as a pond, river, lake, or ocean, or show them a picture of one. Hand them a measuring cup and ask them if they think they could measure all the water. Read them Isaiah 40:12, that God "has measured the waters in the hollow of his hand."
- Take your children to a large hill or show them a picture of mountains. Hand them a scale and ask if they could place that hill or mountain on it and see what it weighs. Read them the ending of Isaiah 40:12, that God has "weighed the mountains in scales and the hills in a balance."
- Take your children where you can see a clear night sky full of stars or show them a picture of a star-filled night sky and ask them to count each star. Read them Psalm 147:4, that God "determines the number of the stars; he gives to all of them their names."

- Explain to your children that God is not only an artist but also an expert in math and science. In fact, he is the one who wrote all the rules for math and science! He has designed the world perfectly to support our lives so that we can learn more about him through everything he has made.
- Read Matthew 22:37 to your children. Ask them what they think it means to "love the Lord your God . . . with all your mind." Explain to them that God wired our brains for intelligence. He wants us to use our minds to learn more about him through science and nature and to gently and creatively share those truths with others.

## See God in Nature

Take your children to a natural area. It can be the woods, a river, a beach, anywhere with a lot of different natural materials. Ask them to go find something they really like, then to bring it back to you, but only through words. Tell them to report back and tell you things such as:

- How big is it? Show me with your hands.
- What is its texture? Soft, smooth, solid, rough?
- What colors does it have?
- Does it smell like anything?
- What did you find around it?
- What is it doing? Swaying? Drooping? Singing? Stretching?

Once your children have given detailed descriptions, go with them to see what they have found. Encourage them in the accurate description they gave, and share a few more descriptors they could have used. This will help them broaden their vocabulary for how to see and define things. Next, it's your turn! Go find something fun to describe to them, and let them take a turn guessing.

# Nature-Minded: Growing a Healthy Mindset Outdoors

*Given a chance, a child will bring the confusion of the world to the woods, wash it in the creek, turn it over to see what lives on the unseen side of that confusion.*

RICHARD LOUV

HAVE YOU EVER EXPERIENCED THE hush of a forest? It is something quieter than silence. While silence is the absence of noise, the quiet of the outdoors introduces a new octave—a stillness enunciated by nature's songs. You can hear it from birds harmonizing from branches, in the wind stirring up grasses, and in a fresh blanket of snow creating an amphitheater of focused acoustics. This quiet is more than an absence of society's noise—it is full. The fullest kind of quiet. Spending time outdoors you can say along with King David in Psalm 131:2, "I have calmed and quieted my soul."

I experienced this level of quiet on an October day as my husband and I gathered our children around us on a dirt road.

"This is going to be a silent hike," my husband explained. "We need to practice self-control, so please, no words."

Before long, I had to separate our two oldest boys after they proved unwilling to subdue their conversations.

A doe mule deer crossed the field, eyeing us curiously before disappearing into the trees. Wandering farther, a speckle-bellied flicker woodpecker darted to and from a lodgepole pine tree.

After exploring for over a mile, my husband whispered a question, "Ok, what direction do you think the car is in?" Our kids and I silently raised our arms and pointed in different directions.

"What did we walk through on our way here?" he asked. Eventually, the kids narrowed it down to the answer he was looking for: a meadow with an animal trail.

"So we know if we find that meadow, we'll know which direction the road is. If we know where the road is, we can follow it back to the car."

He continued with an impromptu lesson on wilderness navigation, along with what to do if they ever become lost.

"Stay put," he instructed. "If you become lost, never keep walking. Instead, find the closest clearing and stay there, call for help, and listen carefully for other humans who can help. Someone will always come looking for you."

After an hour and a half, we returned to the car. Our silent hike was packed with words that matter: intentional whispers of whereabouts, lessons, and discoveries. More importantly, it consisted of quiet moments listening to the woods and the One who spoke them into place.

Walking quietly will be a practice in patience for your children. Begin small with instructions like, "Let's walk without words until we get to that next tree. Listen to the birds' songs as we walk. What do you think they are singing about?" As your children develop this habit, they'll begin hearing more clearly the voice of God amid his creation. They'll develop habits of clearing their minds from distraction and meditating on God's goodness and beauty.

## Is Meditation Biblical?

What do you picture when you think of meditation? It is a concept that looks different across the world. Many modern methods are influenced by false religions and self-serving ambitions. But we can see an original and biblical practice of meditation throughout Scripture. God uses the beauty, quiet, and calm of nature to help us and our children practice his methods of mindful thinking.

"We need to go on a hike to help us sort our minds," my son once told me. It was the summer he was turning nine, and I saw how time outdoors was shaping his perspective.

On a family hike the spring before, he told me how he loves "pressing deep into the woods." I imagine he experiences the same freedom I have when the wilderness untangles our thoughts and sets them straight. I'm sure he senses this much sooner than I do out on the trails.

The woods have a larger task at hand when it comes to sorting my thoughts, purging them from the unnecessary burden, and lightening the mental load I've carried throughout the week. It usually takes at least two miles of hiking before I begin thinking straight. There is a particular milestone on each hike when a shift happens. Unencumbered by tasks and to-dos, I'm free to focus on Philippians 4:8: "Whatever is true, whatever is honorable, whatever is just, whatever is pure, whatever is lovely, whatever is commendable, if there is any excellence, if there is anything worthy of praise, think about these things." My thoughts turn toward all that is lovely and true as I meditate on God's goodness.

In many ways, the concept of meditation has been hijacked by the media and influenced by Eastern practices. The word *meditate* might cause some friction in your spirit—I know it has in mine. Going back to Scripture, however, we discover a biblical definition of *meditation* referring to an acute focus on and study of God's Word and ways. While many people wander into the woods for meditative purposes, the world's idea of meditation is much different and falls short of the biblical definition. Society's focus in meditation is commonly emptying one's mind, while Scripture urges us to fill our minds.

Psalm 1 speaks of the person who is like a tree firmly planted by streams of water, prospering and bearing fruit in season. Verse 2 says, "His delight is in the law of the LORD, and on his law he meditates day and night."

Joshua 1:8 instructs, "This Book of the Law shall not depart from your mouth, but you shall meditate on it day and night, so that you may be careful to do according to all that is written in it. For then you will make your way prosperous, and then you will have good success."

Psalm 77:12 reads, "I will ponder all your work, and meditate on your mighty deeds." Interestingly, the word used in these passages for *meditate* has also been used in Scripture for *study*, such as in Joshua 1:8, "Always remember what is written in the Book of the Teachings. *Study* it day and night to be sure to obey everything that is written there. If you do this, you will be wise and successful in everything" (NCV, emphasis added). It is not passive emptying, but active gathering.

You can practice biblical meditation by filling up on the thoughts of Christ and thinking God's thoughts after him. An excellent place to practice this is out in God's creation, where reflections of his creativity and goodness abound.

Society presents meditation as an act of mindfulness, which ironically can be very far from a full mind. Instead, it focuses on emptying one's mind. An empty mind is not healthy or safe for us or our kids. Recently, when my sons asked me about meditation as the world practices it, I told them. "When our minds are empty, we are vulnerable. Satan can plant thoughts there. Instead, we want to clear our minds to focus on God. We can fill our minds with his thoughts."

One dictionary defines *mindfulness* as this: "a technique in which one focuses one's full attention only on the present, experiencing thoughts, feelings, and sensations but not judging them."[1]

That feels like a far cry from King David's heartfelt plea in Psalm 139:23–24:

> Search me, O God, and know my heart!
> Try me and know my thoughts!
> And see if there be any grievous way in me,
> and lead me in the way everlasting!

Then there is society's focusing "one's full attention only on the present." You might be familiar with popular sayings like "Be in the moment" or "Stay in the present." It's true that God wants us to be aware of and wise with our limited time, like we see in Psalm 90:12: "So teach us to number our days that we may get a heart of wisdom." When we focus *only* on the present moment, however, we miss what really matters: an eternal perspective.

Society says: Focus on the present. Focus on yourself. Don't judge yourself.

God says: Focus on eternity. Love God and others. Align your heart's desires with God's.

We can help our children sift their thoughts, purging what is impure, harmful, or distracting until they are left standing face-to-face with God's truth and can align their thoughts with his agenda.

When we take our kids into nature, we don't *only* want the benefit nature provides of clearing our minds. Like my son said so eloquently, nature can sort our minds. We aim to do away with negative thoughts, lies, and distractions. When we've done that, we can then focus on filling our minds with all that is noble, true, lovely, good, noteworthy, and excellent.

"Think on these things," Scripture tells us. Creation helps us do that. When we can tie God's truth and promises to elements in nature, meditation becomes active and biblical. We are filling up on the fullness of Christ, as we read in Colossians 2:9–10 (NASB), "For in Him all the fullness of Deity dwells in bodily form, and in Him you have been made complete." And in Ephesians 3:19, the apostle Paul tells us "to know the love of Christ that surpasses knowledge, that you may be filled with all the fullness of God." Led by the Holy Spirit, directed by Scripture, and inspired by creation, our kids come to know their Maker and match their thoughts with his.

## Filtering Our Thoughts

If you have ever lived in a city with heavy pollution or been affected by a wildfire, you understand the gift of clean air. After the three months we spent with our wildfire, I developed a deep sense of gratitude for fresh air. Unclean air is nearly unbearable and can have lasting negative impacts on our health.

It's a well-known scientific fact that trees filter the air we breathe. They provide the oxygen we need to live. Matthew Sleeth makes this point in his book *Reforesting Faith*. He writes, "Not until the 1770s was the link between trees and breathing discovered. Scientists found that a mouse in a sealed jar with plants inside and placed in sunlight was a happy mouse. They also found that the mouse died if either the sun or the plants were taken away. The sun-plant-animal oxygen connection was discovered."[2] Talk about a convincing argument for having house plants! On the same page, Sleeth shares an image of the "bronchial tree" in the human body that carries air to our lungs. It holds a striking resemblance to an oak tree. Sleeth makes another correlation between trees and the breath that keeps us alive when he points out that God planted a garden directly after breathing life into Adam's nostrils.

We see this progression in Genesis 2:7–8, "Then the Lord God formed the man of dust from the ground and breathed into his nostrils the breath of life, and the man became a living creature. And the Lord God planted a garden in Eden, in the east, and there he put the man whom he had formed." Trees are practical, providing fruit for eating and air for breathing. Oxygen improves cognitive performance. No wonder a walk in the forest improves our mindsets.

When I was fourteen, I discovered this profound mental, spiritual, and physical component of nature. On the brink of entering high school, I was diagnosed with Addison's disease, a rare and potentially fatal autoimmune disorder. My adrenal glands no longer function, leaving my body defenseless against stress. This diagnosis dropped me into a foreign and confusing world of hospital visits, blood draws, and new information that would determine much of my life expectancy and quality.

At that age, I wasn't able to grasp or process a lot of what was going on around me. Yet looking back on that season, what I do see is me outside. I spent drawn-out hours walking along nature paths throughout our town and surrounding areas. John Muir once wrote, "Everybody needs beauty as well as bread, places to play in and pray in, where Nature may heal and cheer and give strength to body and soul alike."[3] Time spent outdoors filtered my thoughts and brought healing to my body and spirit.

On a recent hike, my son was thinking about our old neighborhood and friends he'd left behind when we moved six months earlier. He normally doesn't show his emotions, but the wilderness invited him to feel all those big feelings.

I held back with him on the trail, comforting him and explaining why we'd chosen to move and our intentional choice to surround him with friends from church, our homeschool group, and our hiking group who share our values.

As much as I wanted to keep explaining our reasoning, my husband encouraged me to just let our son think about these things as we hiked. I was grateful this conversation happened out in the woods, and as we continued our hike, I prayed silently that God would use the woods to help my son sort and filter his thoughts.

When you sense your children have something important they want to talk about, consider taking a walk or hike. Let nature help with the hard conversations.

Our kids will face many uncertain and difficult things in life. We can prepare them with resilience and a healthy filter for their thoughts by spending time in creation. When hard times come and they need to sort their thoughts, may the great outdoors be where they go.

## Renewing Our Minds

Raising kids in uncertain times, it's easy to be overwhelmed by the trials they face and the challenges and threats we know they will encounter growing up. At times we can feel hopeless and out of control.

When the author of Romans talks about our struggle against sin, he points to the enemy's attack on our minds. Romans 7:22–23 says, "For I delight in the law of God, in my inner being, but I see in my members another law *waging war against the law of my mind* and making me captive to the law of sin that dwells in my members" (emphasis added).

What does all this legalese or "law talk" mean?

When we know and follow Christ, we are secure in his salvation. Nothing can shake our position with him. We delight in his life-giving ways. But while we're still living on this broken earth, we will struggle against sin, which often goes hand in hand with doubt. We doubt God's promises, so we compromise. Sin enters, and it pokes holes in the fabric of our faith. Where does this passage say the enemy begins when he wants to uproot our faith? In our minds. Sin is "waging war against the law of my mind." Read: sin attacks what we know to be true,

Perhaps this is why we find passages like 1 Peter 1:13 which instructs, "Therefore, *preparing your minds for action, and being sober-minded*, set your hope fully on the grace that will be brought to you at the revelation of Jesus Christ" (emphasis added). And in Luke 10:27 we read: "You shall love the Lord your God with all your heart and with all your soul and with all your strength *and with all your mind*" (emphasis added).

This is an intellectual faith. It is not built from "hope for" sand. Instead, it is cemented in fact. It stands strong against the enemy's attacks on our thought life. In breaking away from the mainstream thought patterns of this world, we forge new pathways. It becomes easier to "take every thought captive to obey Christ," as 2 Corinthians 10:5 instructs. As our kids diverge from this world's distractions and futility to focus on all that is lovely and true, they will live out Romans 12:2, "Do not be conformed to this world, but be transformed by the renewal of your mind, that by testing you may discern what is the will of God, what is good and acceptable and perfect."

Nature serves as a defense for our children's minds against negative, harmful, and false thoughts.

As parents, bringing our kids outside provides an incredible offensive and defensive opportunity. We are filling their minds with the thoughts of Christ. We are showing our children what true and lasting beauty looks like. We are placing before them matters of truth that cannot be denied. They are encountering irreproachable evidence for God. In playing outside together, we give them a sieve with which to sift their thoughts. We are not telling them what to think. Instead, we are giving them the tools they need to think critically. We are preparing them for life, all while picking wildflowers and skipping stones.

## Step Outside

Do you know what your children are thinking right now? Are you aware of their current struggles with friends, growing up, school, family, or other questions about life? As our kids grow older, it becomes increasingly difficult to discern what they're up against and how to help them. Taking them outside is an incredibly effective way of helping them sort out their thoughts and questions. In a society where mental illness, anxiety, and depression are sky-high, nature provides a sanctuary for our kids. Give your children every opportunity to fix their minds on all that is lovely and true by taking them outside as often as possible. God does not let his Word return void, and he speaks his Word loudly through nature. By sharing God's promises and nature's beauty with your children, their minds will become more resilient against darkness, and they will learn to recognize and live in the light of God's truth.

### See Nature in the Bible

- Read to your children Psalm 1:1–3 and Jeremiah 17:7–8. Perhaps write them on three-by-five-inch cards and memorize them over the next few weeks.
- Ask your children what they think are ways to "meditate" or think upon God's Word. If they need help, guide them to answers like singing God's Word, reading God's Word, telling others about God's goodness, and spending time in God's creation. An excellent resource for singing God's Word is the "Hidden In My Heart" Scripture music series by Scripture Lullabies. You can find their music at www.scripture-lullabies.com.
- Read to your children Philippians 4:8, "Whatever is true, whatever is honorable, whatever is just, whatever is pure, whatever is lovely, whatever is commendable, if there is any excellence, if there is anything worthy of praise, think about these things." Write down the qualities mentioned in this verse: True. Honor-

able. Just. Pure. Lovely. Commendable. Excellent. Praiseworthy. Help your children think of and list things under each quality. Here are some examples: What is lovely? A flower. A butterfly. A rabbit. What is just? Helping and standing up for others. Taking care of God's creation. What is excellent? A perfectly ripe strawberry. What is pure? God's love. Snow falling from the sky.

*See God in Nature*

On your calendar, set aside a day within the next two weeks to take your children to a nearby river, stream, or pond, one with trees or foliage at its edge. Wintertime works as well, even if the water is frozen. An iced-over river provides a great visual for how water sustains trees even in harsh conditions. Don't worry about curating the perfect educational experience. Instead, take your time exploring and playing in the area while casually discussing the following points:

- Refer to Psalm 1:1–3 and Jeremiah 17:7–8. Ask your children how God's Word is like water to us. If they need help, guide them to answers such as it feeds our roots, keeps us alive, and helps us grow and live well.
- Ask your children: "Do you think these trees would grow as well in the desert without water?"
- Ask your children to be quiet for two minutes with you and sit in silence by the water's edge. Encourage them to close their eyes and listen to the songs of creation, then share what you heard.

# — 8 —

# Native Pastimes

*It takes time—loose, unstructured dreamtime—to
experience nature in a meaningful way.*

RICHARD LOUV

TODAY'S CHILD SPENDS AN AVERAGE of six hours in front of a screen
and a mere six minutes outside each day.[1] Our kids are growing up in
a very different technological world than we did. I'm sure you, like
me, want your children to spend time in wholesome ways but struggle against technology's pull on their attention. Through time outdoors, we can revive our kids' allure with God's creation and instill
in them a healthy balance in how they spend their time.

This is what my family was pursuing one day as we played at the
Rio Blanco river in the Rocky Mountains.

"Mama, that one got away." My three-year-old daughter stood
beside the river, toes submerged in the cold current. From her hand,
a branch-turned-fishing-rod dangled over the water.

"It's ok; another is swimming up," she assured me. We passed
the time as we waited for my husband and three sons to meet up

with us. An hour before, we had dropped them off upriver with the canoe.

"I'm making breakfast," my daughter narrated her play to me. One flat stone served as her plate, piled high with "salad" leaves foraged from nearby bushes.

I looked up from my book right in time to see a yellow warbler fly from a willow patch on one side of the river to the other. Its olive-green-tinged wings and quick, swooping flight gave away its identification. A moment later, a kingfisher let out its high-pitched clicking song. They are my favorite bird, and my gaze snapped to the sky in time to see him flying downriver.

The men wrapped around the final curve of the river. They approached quickly with wide grins. I imagined young Meriwether Lewis and William Clark looking much like my own boys at that moment, the spirit of discovery thick and palpable, like a dewy fog refreshing the earth.

Isn't this how time is meant to be spent? It can be a morning floating on the river or hours given to unplanned play in the woods. Some days it's an afternoon in the meadow or an evening picnic at the park. So long as it is outdoors, surrounded by beauty to spark your children's curiosity, it's time well invested and never regretted.

Time in nature is accessible to each of us. Depending on where you live, it might be more challenging to spend time outdoors. It looks different from place to place. Yet I have heard time and again of families making the outdoors a priority even in urban settings. It comes down to the habits and rhythms we create as families.

From our children's first years toddling around our one-acre yard on the outskirts of Kansas City, my husband and I knew that we needed to provide them valuable chunks of time outdoors. As we stepped outside, we witnessed their spirits coming alive.

I count it a sweet gift of God that while they were yet so young—crawling across the garden patch on all fours and plucking tender beans from vines with plump toddler hands—he showed me the power of time in nature. With babies still on my hips and in my belly, I couldn't have foreseen the challenges we'd face as they grew up, or how nature's lessons would equip us to face each obstacle.

Years later, with our oldest eleven years old, I can see how God was training our eyes, minds, and spirits toward beautiful things. Doing so, he prepares us for the temptations, distractions, and deceptions our kids will encounter and equips us to help them navigate rough waters.

As our children grow up, the allure and enticement of society grow all the stronger. Can you see your children's attention divided in dozens of ways? Are you happy with how your children spend their time? Personally, there is always room for improvement in my home.

Thankfully, there is plenty of grace and help for this endeavor. As we take our kids outside—away from interruptions—God's handiwork commands their attention. In a noisy world bent on winning their affections, we can recenter our children's hearts and minds by surrounding them with God's creativity. Through many exposures in nature, their minds begin renegotiating what's important and how they want to spend their days.

In Acts 14 we find encouragement for turning away—and helping our kids turn away—from vain and useless things. In verses 15-17, the apostle Paul urged his listeners:

> Why are you doing these things? We also are men, of like nature with you, and we bring you good news, that you should turn from these vain things to a living God, who made the heaven and the earth and the sea and all that is in them. In past generations he allowed all the nations to walk in their own ways. Yet he did not leave himself without witness, for he did good by giving you rains from heaven and fruitful seasons, satisfying your hearts with food and gladness.

In the passage above, we see "vain things" contrasted by a living God who made "the heaven and the earth and the sea and all that is in them." God used rains from heaven and fruitful seasons as reminders of what's important in life. He's using nature in the same way today to help our families live for what matters. As we take our kids outside to explore creation, they will recognize God's gifts and trade vain or worthless activities for ones that feed their souls.

## Invasive Pastimes Choke the Ecosystem of Our Souls

Think about the difference between your childhood and that of your children. What new challenges, threats, or temptations face your children that you never had to worry about as a kid? I remember receiving my first flip phone at age thirteen. I felt like the coolest kid on the block because not only could it send and receive calls, but it could take photos. Holding it in my hand, I could never have imagined how technology would progress in just one generation, and that this little phone and what it represented would become one of the biggest challenges of my parenthood.

Our kids have a buffet of useless things set before them every day. The media invests countless dollars attempting to win and keep our kids' attention and allegiance. But what affect is it having on their minds, bodies, and souls? If your children behave differently after spending a morning playing video games compared to a morning outdoors, it might be a strong indicator of what's better for them. The challenge, of course, is this: vain and useless things lay at our children's fingertips. Worthless pursuits abound, encroaching all the more as our children grow older. It's a lot like an invasive weed overtaking native plants. Invasive species are plants that don't belong on a landscape. They've been brought in from foreign places whether by people or by seed carried on the wind or by insects and birds. They choke the life from an ecosystem. Many of these invasive species trick onlookers with their aesthetics and paint an area with deceptive beauty. Standing beside a densely foliaged hillside, few will understand that these beautiful plants pose a threat. We have to consider what types of invasive plants might be lurking in our children's days and activities. Is there a threat to how they're spending their childhood?

As invasive plant species were brought in from across oceans to lend exotic beauty and variation to our gardens and landscapes, they began to spread into natural areas. Douglas W. Tallamy explains, "About 85 percent of invasive woody plant species in the United States are escapees from our gardens."[2] Considering that an invasive tree can support a handful of insect species while a native tree can support several hundred insect species—which then go on to feed our birds and animals—the progression of invasive plants at the expense of native plants is devastating to ecosystems.

I see the same thing happening with the landscape of childhood. Like the recent introduction of invasive plants, the recent escalation of technology and media has created a dangerous fascination. Time given to devices crowds out other activities. Just like our assumptions about beautiful plants doing minimal damage, we may think a video game or movie is harmless. It seems wholesome and keeps our children's attention. Perhaps it even helps them stay out of trouble. But it quickly moves from harmless to invasive, monopolizing time and attention. It crowds out native or natural pastimes, or how God meant for us to spend time: in creation, with family and friends, creating, in purposeful work, and enjoying his good gifts.

In my research around invasive plants, several things struck me. Let's look at them and compare the list to the ecosystems of our children's souls:

1. **It is a recent problem,** resulting from overseas plants introduced in the past couple of centuries.
2. **These actions were well-intentioned,** and we were caught off guard by the adverse effects.

3. **Invasive plants have the upper hand on a landscape.** None of their natural predators that would keep them at bay and under control back home exist here. With free rein of the landscape, they thrive.

4. **Native (belonging) plants are highly vulnerable and at a disadvantage.** Native plants are forced out and lose their claim on the land as invasive plants overcrowd and consume the landscape.

It is similar to the ecosystem of our children's souls.

1. **It is a recent and rapidly developing problem.** As parents, we're encountering new societal pressures like we never have before. This tech age introduces opportunities, threats, and dangers we've never encountered in history. Our own parents might stand back bewildered at what they see or, feeling it's the way the world is going, might hand their grandchild a device without considering what they're giving up or in to. Either way, our own parents perhaps struggle relating to or offering us advice on managing the issue because their generation of parents didn't have to, or at least not to this extent.

2. **Intentions were good. The Results? Not so much.** The rise of tech has in many ways been well-intentioned. Advancements have enabled us to solve problems like never before. Many of these solutions have benefited humanity in magnificent ways. Doctors can heal illnesses that in recent history were deadly. We talk with loved ones worldwide and see their faces in real-time. Education can happen virtually anywhere. We can perform jobs remotely, allowing families flexibility and more time together. Yet in the shadow of these achievements lurk devastating threats to our children's hearts, minds, bodies, and souls. An article from *Business Insider* sharing an interview discussion with the late Steve Jobs, CEO of Apple and the inventor of the iPad, shares this:

Steve Jobs in 2010 was on the stage at the Apple event releasing the iPad and he described it as a wonderful device that brought you educational tools. It allowed you to surf the web, it allowed you to watch videos, it allowed you to interact with other people. And he basically said it's the best way to do all those things.

Two years later when he was asked "Your kids must love the iPad?" [h]e said "Actually we don't allow the iPad in the home. We think it's too dangerous for them in effect." The reason why he said that was because he recognized just how addictive the iPad was as a vehicle for delivering things to people. That once you had the iPad in front of you, or when you took it away from the home with you, you'd always have access to these platforms that were very addictive. That were hard to resist.[3]

Simply put, we had no idea how these exciting introductions would wreak havoc on the landscapes of our souls.

3. **Invasive pastimes have the upper hand.** As Steve Jobs believed, the recent infiltration of tech and media has an extreme advantage over our children's attention. They are designed to be addictive. If we fail to train our children to use tech as a tool rather than a toy and to be creators rather than consumers, invasive activities, with little to no eternal significance or benefit to body, mind, and soul, will monopolize our children's days.

In their book *Screen Kids*, authors Gary Chapman and Arlene Pellicane share about the toxicity of screens and phones at a young age: "A phone is like a childhood killer. Once a child gets one, the door of childhood swiftly closes. Old hobbies and imaginary play are left behind for the intoxication of the digital world. Kids stop looking up and around at the world in curiosity—their heads go down and stay down."[4]

Oh, that we would raise an outlier generation of kids keeping their heads up!

As I was writing my book *936 Pennies*, I researched how much time children spend on average in front of a screen or device throughout their 936 weeks of childhood. What I found was disheartening. Between birth and eighteen, children spend an average of 205 *waking* weeks with a device.[5] Roughly 22 percent of childhood is traded for a screen, and this was back in 2017. Knowing these numbers, I couldn't parent the same. We can't leave our homes to a default setting.

The founder of the 1000 Hours Outside movement, Ginny Yurich, compared this to the four to seven minutes on average a child spends each day outdoors, amounting to a few half-hour chunks a week.[6] If we're generous and run with the higher end of seven minutes a day, then the average child spends, from birth to eighteen, 4.55 weeks of their childhood outside. It is an alarming statistic representing 0.48 percent of their youth.

Two hundred five weeks with a screen, 4.55 weeks outside. It's no wonder we've witnessed decreased attention spans, weight gain, plummeting mental health, a decline in social interactions and confidence, and a disconnection from family amongst our newest generations. I am not suggesting that a disconnect from nature and addiction to screens are the sole causes of these issues, but they certainly contribute.

On this topic, Richard Louv coined the term *nature-deficit disorder*. He wrote: "Nature-deficit disorder describes the human costs of alienation from nature, among them: diminished use of the senses, attention difficulties, and higher rates of physical and emotional illnesses. The disorder can be detected in individuals, families, and communities."[7]

Think for a moment about how technology influences your children's mindsets. While there might be some educational benefits, there are certainly some drawbacks and dangers as well. Now consider how nature directs your children's thoughts.

Technology is always progressing, changing, and pressing forward. There is always pressure to "keep up." Nature is steadfast and beckons us back in time. With technology, we can never be current enough. We become proficient just as a new upgrade or platform releases. Nature, although inexhaustible, is dependable. There is always more to learn, but the targets are not moving. Everything points back to a Creator who does not change. While technology often leaves our thoughts blurred and crowded, time outdoors frees us from that burden. It reminds us of what matters.

4. **Native pastimes are at a disadvantage.** To wrap up our comparison of invasive plants to invasive pastimes, the natural inclinations God designed our kids with are incredibly vulnerable in today's society. Children feel left out and even embarrassed if they're not well-versed in the latest video game. They feel ostracized if they don't carry around a smartphone by age ten. Once they step into the world of technology, previous inclinations toward nature, reading, creativity, and physical activities fall prey to screens.

God designed ecosystems in an incredibly complex and intricate manner. When sin broke the world, this engineering became vulnerable. One slight imbalance affects the whole system. The same is true for our kids. We have to ask ourselves if there is a balance we can strike here. Can we bring over exotic plants to lend beauty to our gardens while reserving the majority of our landscapes for native plants, enough of a percentage to support our ecosystems? Can we introduce tech into our kids' lives while keeping it within its boundaries?

This isn't a matter of overhauling our lives. Just as restoring an ecosystem takes time, so does reestablishing a healthy balance for our kids.

But what if you could redeem 4.1 percent of your kids' childhoods with one simple shift? By trading one hour a day of screen time for an hour outside, 4.1 percent of their time is set aside for excellent use. Of course, this number changes depending on how old your children are (and how much of their childhood is already spent), but it is never too late to make these intentional shifts. Every hour spent outside is worthwhile, and God will put it to great use.

On May 30, 2020, I sat in the shade of a massive cottonwood tree in the park by our home. The kids were on a bike ride with their auntie, and I anxiously willed them to round the corner of the bike path and meet me here, beneath this tree, in time. I scanned the park's greenspace looking for their blond-white heads of hair.

I looked back to the text message my dad sent nine minutes before: "Launch in 10!"

I caught the red glint of my youngest son's bike, and I stood up, waving my arms as emphatically as I could. "Hurry! It's launching!"

My sons rushed over and plopped down beside me in the green grass. We huddled over my phone.

"Five . . . Four . . . Three . . ."

We watched, breathless, as the SpaceX Falcon 9 Rocket lit up on a launchpad from NASA's Kennedy Space Center in Florida. Jim Bridenstine, NASA administrator, commented about the event: "Today a new era in human spaceflight begins as we once again launched American astronauts on American rockets from American soil on their way to the International Space Station, our national lab orbiting Earth."[8]

I once listened to my father share a moment much like this. He stood behind a podium at my grandfather's funeral, telling his boyhood story. On July 20, 1969, in Chicago, my dad followed his father through a field, searching for a clear signal on the radio my grandpa held. Once the fizzling split open to a clear transmit, they held their position.

"Two hundred feet." They listened, daring not to take a breath.

"That's good. One hundred and twenty feet . . . One hundred feet . . . Okay. Seventy-five feet. There's looking good . . ."

Fifty-two years later, my sons and I stared unblinking at the screen on my smartphone.

"Two . . . One . . ." The shuttle lifted and propelled itself toward the sky. Our breaths held.

In a field decades before, my father waited, holding his breath and listening to Neil Armstrong's voice from the moon, "Houston, Tranquility Base here. The Eagle has landed."

My boys waited for the shuttle's trails to disappear into the sky, then immediately turned toward the green space, running for trees to climb. They spent three minutes with the screen on my phone and witnessed a historical moment, then returned to their afternoon outside. We struck a healthy balance that day. There was reason and purpose behind our time with a device. Tech was not invasive. Instead, my children's natural inclinations toward play and exploration won them over.

## Nurturing Our Children's Interests

We still have a chance at childhoods that favor outdoor play over screen time. We must go outside frequently and long enough to identify what out in nature will win our children over. What will absorb their attention? What will reconnect them with the innate sense of wonder God placed in them while they were still in the womb? For my children the past several years, it has been rocks. A whole lot of rocks.

Considering my boys' room full of fossils and their growing intrigue with precious gemstones and minerals, I checked out a stack of geology books from the library, picture books packed with bright, detailed illustrations and descriptions of every kind of rock.

On a beautiful Friday morning in October, we drove to a nearby trail along the river. Branches of cottonwoods stubbornly clung to their final golden leaves. Most had drifted to the forest floor or floated down the river. A female mallard duck glided through the water, parting autumn leaves with her feathered breast.

"How would you describe this area to someone?" My husband, a compass dangling from his hand, posed the question to our boys.

"It's along the river, by the big bridge," our oldest painted together a description with words. They set to work drawing a compass rose on grid paper, marking North. Two perpendicular lines mirrored the bridge to our left. They drew careful, winding blue lines for the river. A gray pencil marked the rocky shore. Yellow depicted the golden willow bushes clinging to the riverbanks.

"Think about anything you might need on your map to signify where you find rocks," I instructed. The boys added narrow-leafed cottonwood trees, a large pile of driftwood, and a thin spit of rocky shore jutting out into the river, dividing the water.

I began guiding them. "Ok, now that you have your map, here's what you'll do. We have bags labeled one through twelve. You get to explore the area you've mapped and find twelve rocks. You'll put them each into a numbered bag and label them on your map with the corresponding number where you found each rock. Then you'll write a description of the area where you located each rock."

The boys set straight to work searching for rocks, labeling them on their map, and writing detailed descriptions of their search areas.

"These are skills you can use in a lot of neat careers," I told them.

My oldest agreed, telling me he wants to grow up and get a job helping people locate fossils.

This careful collection of natural things is helping me to see like a child again. While my children are naturally drawn to the dimples and curvatures in a rock, I have to look much more carefully and allow the blue sky, waving willows, and driftwood traveling downriver to lift my thoughts from whatever muck they've settled in. Then I can notice the rocks and the stories they tell. Aldo Leopold once called it "a refined taste in natural objects."[9] Our children have refined tastes. Their observation is careful and acute. A natural curiosity compels them, and our only job is to nurture and protect their interests.

When we returned home, I pulled out a wooden box with a sliding lid, placed their numbered rocks inside, and taped their grid map to the top. My children have a lot of these boxes, collections of natural things strewn about the house. Some I know of, some I have yet to discover. One day I walked into their room to a peculiar smell I could not place. I soon discovered containers of water lining their shelf. One hosted snails. Another had water beetles from the creek down the road. They were exhibits to be studied and admired before release. Another day, I braved the task of cleaning out under my middle son's bed. Along with Lego bricks, books, and an Oreo cookie (minus the cream), I discovered prairie dog skulls and bones from the field next to our home.

Have you ever noticed your children's inclination to collect things from nature? Maybe you, like me, have pulled stones from pockets before loading the laundry machine or found bird feathers between book pages. These mementos serve as visual anchors for our kids' memories. What we see as ordinary, they see as exceptional. In the sixteenth century, it wasn't only children taking part in these outdoor scavenger hunts. A peculiar hobby began emerging across European homes. Adults built collections of natural wonders, dubbed *Wunderkammer* (Cabinets of Wonder), also known as "Curiosity Cabinets." Many times, these in-home museums served the purpose of entertainment or acted as a status symbol. Whatever the motive, however, the result was phenomenal: adults gaping in amazement and sharing in conversations around things found in nature.

I experienced this firsthand when our boys hosted their second Neighborhood Fossil Museum. This follow-up event to their inaugural spring museum added an additional attraction: excavation tours guided by my middle and youngest boys every hour. I watched from our front lawn as my sons guided groups of children and adults around our field, trailing a red wagon full of gloves and shovels. Several times I looked out to see museumgoers of every age sitting and digging in the dirt. They returned with the wagon full of fossils—mostly clamshells—preserved in time. A favorite find of the day included an embedded spiral shell. Visitors proudly took home their treasures.

One of the museumgoers was our geologist neighbor, Paul, from our previous neighborhood. He has long inspired our sons' infatuation with rocks and what geology can tell us. The boys love when Paul comes to their museum events because he helps them identify some of the stones they've yet to find names for.

"I know what this is," Paul said, picking up a small, round, flat fossil with a perfect hole in the center. It resembled a wheel.

"This is a ring from the stalk of a crinoid," he explained, pulling up a picture of it on his phone. It was an exact match to our fossil.

Aldo Leopold, in *A Sand County Almanac*, shared a story of these crinoid finds. He wrote about a fossil collector by the name of Charles Wachsmuth who, with the assistance of his colleague Frank Springer, turned an ordinary in-home museum into a world-renowned collection. Leopold wrote:

> When I was a boy, there was an old German merchant who lived in a little cottage in our town. On Sundays he used to go out and knock chips off the limestone ledges along the Mississippi, and he had a great tonnage of these chips, all labeled and catalogued. The chips contained little fossil stems of some defunct water creatures called crinoids. The townspeople regarded this gentle old fellow as just a little bit abnormal, but harmless. One day the newspaper reported the arrival of certain titled strangers. It was whispered that these visitors were great scientists. Some of them were from foreign lands, and some among the world's leading paleontologists.

They came to visit the harmless old man, and to hear his pronouncements on crinoids, and they accepted these pronouncements as law. When the old German died, the town awoke to the fact that he was a world authority on his subject, a creator of knowledge, a maker of scientific history. . . . His collection went to a national museum, and his name is known in all the nations of the earth.[10]

Later in the book, Leopold tells the story of Margaret Morse Nice, a homemaker in Ohio.[11] In her yard, she began placing different colored bands around the legs of common house sparrows to identify individual birds. For over ten years, she studied these feathered visitors to her yard. After a decade of lay observations, "she knew more about sparrow society, sparrow politics, sparrow economics, and sparrow psychology than anyone had ever learned about any bird. Science beat a path to her. Ornithologists of all nations seek her counsel."[12]

I do not doubt that our children—mine, yours, and an entire outlying group of this generation—can leave these kinds of marks on history. I want so badly to peek into the childhoods of the old German man and Ohio housewife. Were they allowed chunks of time outside? Were they encouraged to follow their outdoor obsessions and learn all they could about a particular thing that caught their interest? I'm guessing so. I want to sit down with their parents and learn all I can from them. But mostly, I want to take from these stories the promise that we can raise our kids to preserve these connections with the natural world. This society is not too far gone. We can shift the trajectory of what an average childhood looks like, and it all begins with how we choose to spend our time.

An intrigue with natural wonders is present in each of our kids. It may be difficult to see or believe from your current vantage point. Busyness, ingrained habits, and invasive pastimes may cloud your vision. You may look at your children and yearn for them to experience this wonder but fear the connection is severed. They may seem disinterested. But God has placed the potential for this connection within each of us. Look intently for that note of interest, a glimmer of fascination. Is it birds? Insects? Trees? Mammals? Aquatic life? Outer space? The river, lake, or ocean? Caves? Forest? Desert? Is it rocks, minerals, and fossils? What ignites a question in their minds for which they are desperate and driven to find an answer?

Like a paleontologist, you may have to work hard to unearth your children's interests in nature, but unlike a paleontologist, we get to bring an old thing back to life!

## Restoring What Once Was Lost

Rather than a fossil forgotten in time, the connection between children and nature is more like an exhausted or neglected ecosystem. This is good news, because you have the opportunity to restore your children's (and your) sense of curiosity and wonder!

On a summer morning, I stood on a dirt path along the river that runs through town, overlooking a thriving wetland. A decade before, it was nothing but a pit of rocks, exploited as a gravel mine and trashed with forgotten vehicles and rubbish. The path wound between the river and several ponds. The riverbanks were built unnaturally high during the mining, preventing spring's rising river waters from feeding the ponds. As a result, aquatic creatures could no longer travel from river to pond or from pond to river. Corridors for these creatures were destroyed, and the ecosystem of both the river and ponds suffered devastating effects. But then ecologists and conservationists stepped in. The riverbanks were lowered to their original heights. Water flowed again from the river to the ponds. After a decade of restoration efforts, we're just beginning to see a response from wildlife. Chokeberry trees and wild sumac are growing. Cattails sway along the pond's perimeter. Three entire acres of wetlands have been restored. Riparian birds are returning. What once looked too far gone and hopeless is now a hopeful, living, growing, progressing ecosystem.

It is not too late for our kids. It will take time and effort, but every moment we spend outdoors with them matters. It is all lending to a beautiful ecosystem of the soul. Looking back on these years, we'll see a path of time well spent—the way God intended a childhood to unfold.

## *Step Outside*

Nature provides us an excellent segue for our kids' childhoods. It acts as a smooth and inviting transition for how they choose to spend their time. Instead of a hard jolt or cold-turkey strategy of cutting off media, nature offers a gentler approach for reducing screen time and replacing it with exploration and adventure. Your children will be encouraged by your willingness to step outside alongside them.

As you notice what their attention is drawn to, linger there with them. Encourage them in their outdoor pursuits. Bring friends along and make time outdoors as free and enjoyable as possible. God will not let any of this go to waste. Each time you step outside will bear fruit for your children and will create a thriving landscape in their soul.

### See Nature in the Bible

Children often live nearsighted. They are focused on what is immediately in front of them. This can be an advantage as they're more inclined to enjoy time while not worrying about tomorrow. But we can develop our children's sense of time in a biblical manner by helping them embrace an eternal perspective. Read your children the Scriptures below and use the discussion points to guide them into deeper understanding:

- Isaiah 40:8 (NCV): "The grass dies and the flowers fall, but the word of our God will live forever." Everything we see in nature will eventually end, but God will make all things new and even more beautiful! And what will never end is his Word. We can trust everything the Bible says and that it is true forever.

- Isaiah 54:10 (NCV): "The mountains may disappear, and the hills may come to an end, but my love will never disappear; my promise of peace will not come to an end." God is timeless. It's hard to imagine, but he has no beginning and no end. This is one thing that makes him God! That means everything about him is timeless, including his love. He has always loved us, and he always will love us.

- Matthew 6:19–21 (NCV): "Don't store treasures for yourselves here on earth where moths and rust will destroy them and thieves can break in and steal them. But store your treasures in heaven where they cannot be destroyed by moths or rust and where thieves cannot break in and steal them. Your heart will be where your treasure is." Because God is eternal and he invites us to live forever with him, he wants us to live right now by thinking about eternity. When this verse talks about "treasure," it doesn't mean only our money. How can we give our time, energy, attention, and work to things that affect people forever? We can live bigger lives than what we see here on earth. By spending our time God's way, we can affect eternity!

### See God in Nature

God values time in creation and community. A great way to encourage your children's outdoor interests is by getting friends involved. If your children aren't accustomed to spending hours outside, they might need a little bit of peer motivation. Also, when reducing something like screen time, it often helps to focus not on what they're losing. Avoid language like "we're going to spend less time on your devices." Instead focus on what they're gaining: "We're going to go play with friends at the creek today!"

Chances are there are daily hiking groups near you. You can also join nature programs and classes. Your local city, natural areas department, or nature center should have information online as to what is available. Find opportunities for your children to engage with nature alongside other children who enjoy doing the same.

I lead a local hiking group where families hike together twice a month. We hike two to four miles with plenty of breaks to snack and play, and we enjoy ten-minute nature lessons. Time and again I hear statements like these from parents:

- We would have never known this trail was here if we weren't in this group.
- My child would never hike like this if it was only us. They hike so much farther with friends.
- My child would be complaining about hiking if they didn't have friends to play with along the trail.
- They enjoy a little healthy competition to hike as far as their friends do.

After spending time outdoors with friends, casually ask your children questions like these:

- What do you think made this time extra special?
- Did you enjoy discovering things with your friends?
- What kinds of games, challenges, or adventures did you and your friends think of out there?
- Where would you like to explore next time with your friends?
- Do you think nature is an important piece of building friendships and enjoying time how God wants us to?

— 9 —

# Nature's Time Capsule

*As if you could kill time without injuring eternity.*
HENRY DAVID THOREAU

THERE IS A TERM WE do not use in our home: *killing time.*

Why, after all, would we want to slay our most precious commodity? If you've felt time slipping through your fingers like sand in an hourglass, I'm sure you share these sentiments. Our kids are growing up right before our eyes, and we want *more* time.

In my first book, *936 Pennies: Discovering the Joy of Intentional Parenting*, I shared a story of a mason jar filled with pennies. It was a challenge wrapped in gift form, presented to us at our one-year-old son's child dedication service at church.

"Every penny in this jar represents one week with your child from birth to eighteen," our pastor explained. Suddenly, that jar felt a whole lot heavier in my hands. My husband and I could visualize our son's childhood and grasp how fleeting time truly is. If we are not careful, it is carried away on the wind like dandelion seeds on a summer's afternoon.

159

Our pastor challenged us to remove one penny every week and consider how we spent that time. As parents we need to ask ourselves these questions often: Are we intentionally investing in our kids' childhoods? Are we building into their legacies and impacting their eternities? Are there connection points where we reconvened with our children, looked them in the eyes, and spent undistracted time with them?

It took me a while to begin counting out pennies from that jar. Perhaps your heart already aches at how quickly these years are passing. But there is a reward from this practice. Psalm 90:12 (NIV) says, "Teach us to number our days, that we may gain a heart of wisdom." Counting out a penny each week grants us a heart of wisdom. We glean insight into how to best spend these days.

It wasn't long after we began counting pennies that God revealed to us nature's ability to slow time down. Naturally, every parent longs for this superpower, to restrain the hands on a clock face and to tame time.

There's a common saying, often attributed to Corrie Ten Boom, "If the devil cannot make you sin, he'll make you busy."[1] Have you seen this in your own home? The strain of too much activity, too many obligations, too much spending, too many hours spent in traffic, too many commitments, and too many expectations build like a pressure cooker until an inevitable explosion occurs. If the enemy wants a handle on our families, he will make us busy. Too busy for reading together. Too busy to play outside. Too busy for family walks. Too busy for dinner together around the table. Too busy for God.

At "too busy," the enemy has us in the palm of his grimy hands. Rushing swallows moments and absorbs our best intentions. Rushing cripples memories from being made with our children.

Alternatively, refusing to rush allows us a unique advantage in life, simply because no one else is doing it, so it seems. By practicing a cultural revolt and taking back control of our lives and homes, we can experience family life in a powerful way that most others are missing out on. As we do, we might just create a ripple effect. We have an intuitive ache to make these years with our kids matter. Stepping outside, we discover it is possible through the lens of nature.

## Seeing Time Through the Lens of Nature

In his book *24/6*, Matthew Sleeth shares, "Time changes when viewed through different lenses."[2] Nature is one of those lenses. It alters how we view life and time.

I previously mentioned Ginny Yurich's 1000 Hours Outside movement. After our family embraced a nature-filled lifestyle, I realized that these one thousand hours are compounding. They are far more valuable than one thousand focused hours spent elsewhere because their dividends are exponential. Every hour outside affects the hour after it—and even before it—by changing our perspective and granting clarity.

It is similar to my family's practice of *Shabbat*, the Hebrew word for Sabbath, which can mean "to stop and delight." Once a week, we stop everything, put all work away, and spend a day delighting in life. We read, play board games, go on walks, ride bikes, chat with neighbors, create, and dream. We don't drive anywhere or spend money, and we put away our screens. We remember what life is for. What I quickly found upon embracing Sabbath is that the one day a week given to rest and delight seeps into the other six days. It is the same with every hour spent outside. It influences how we spend the rest of our time. Put simply, we cheat time. Or maybe more accurately, we cooperate with it. It is no longer a thing ripping the rug from beneath our best intentions. Instead, we work in harmony with the limits God places on our lives. We return to a childhood perception of time. Mathew Sleeth said it this way, "When we are young . . . we hear the birds others are too busy to notice. Time seems endless."[3]

## Cementing Memories Through Our Senses

Think back to a profound memory from your childhood. Hold that memory in your mind and play out the scene it holds. What do you see, smell, taste, feel, and hear? God created our senses to hold and unlock memories within our minds. In teaching your children to engage their senses in nature, you can gift them with crisp and clear memories of their outdoor experiences. My firstborn reminded me of this one day at the ponds near our home.

My sons busied themselves at the water's edge. They counted frogs beneath the water, poking their noses above the surface. They watched dragonflies balancing on tall reeds. They followed a four-foot bull snake at a safe distance as it made its way along the rocky beach. I called them over to the park shelter when I noticed a mama barn swallow delivering breakfast to her chicks. Their nest was tucked into a crevice of the shelter's wooden roof.

Hopping on a picnic table, I stretched my arm high above my head, maneuvering the angle of my phone to take a photo. Mama fed her babies, and I grew frustrated as I couldn't capture the shot. The zoom on my phone did no justice as it blurred the sharp lines of the swallow's tail and melded its vibrant rusty orange into its iridescent indigo blue.

"It's ok, Mom," my son told me. "This can just be a memory time."

I slipped my phone back into my pocket and stood side by side with my kids as we watched the swallow family interact. The scene is anchored deeply within my memory reserve because I entered fully into the moment, studying the birds' colors and listening to the chicks' hungry and excited chirping.

Nature has this power. As desperately as we want to capture moments and secure them in our spirits, nature steps beyond our human efforts and capabilities. Nature is a time capsule for our memories because it invites us into a magnificent arena for creating meaningful family connections and secures those experiences within the reservoirs of our souls.

We remember an experience more fully when we partake of it through our sight, touch, smell, sound, and taste. Its details are not lost or obscured.

When I smell the wet, fragrant spring soil, it takes me back to our first home in Kansas City. I am digging in our garden with our two sons, one toddling between bean vines, another crawling straight for the strawberry patch.

When I taste pineapple or a sweet tomato, I am back hiking Hewlett Gulch, where our family spent a day learning to forage. We plucked sun-warmed ground cherries straight from the vine and discovered their sweet, acidic pineappley, tomatoey flavor. Running through a patch of honeysuckle on a summer afternoon, my mind travels to the back yard of our rental home years ago, nursing my newborn daughter beside a patch of honeysuckle and lilac bushes.

When I hear the click-call of a kingfisher, I am back at the river with binoculars slung around my neck, our kids running up ahead with their own binoculars and bird book. We are three hours into our day of bird-watching, counting species across our county.

God wants us to remember these days. It would be a shame to think about looking back on eighteen years of our kids' childhoods and not remembering how we spent them. God has so much more for us. He made our brains capable of creating, anchoring, and retrieving memories. He's given us memory triggers in our senses. Nature utilizes these triggers by lending us a robust collection of scents, sounds, sights, textures, and flavors. As we take advantage of them, we help our kids harness time and experience what's eternal right here on earth.

## What Wildflowers Teach Us About Time

If you were to visit the same natural space every week throughout the spring and summer, you would recognize how wildflowers come and go, and how short-lived a beautiful thing can be.

Some of life's most poignant lessons about time come from wildflowers.

July is prime wildflower season in Colorado, yet most of them go unnoticed. I often wonder how many blossoms, tucked into far-off wilderness corners, never have an audience.

As you spend more time in nature, you will discover that flowers have a cadence. In the areas we explore near our home, bluebell blossoms act as an opening note in the spring. A few years ago, I realized how quickly the bluebells bloomed then disappeared. Nowadays I stop to enjoy them a little longer. Large white yucca flowers are here one day and gone the next. On a summer afternoon as our family wandered through the wilderness, I plucked the tall stalk of a hairy clematis or "sugarbowl" flower with its flashy, deep-violet bloom, and handed it to my daughter. Eyeing patches of them dotting the forest, I knew a month from then they would be drooping white wraiths of past blooms, glory come and gone.

"For we are but of yesterday and know nothing," Job 8:9 reminds us, "for our days on earth are a shadow." Wildflowers stand, stretch, and shift. The sun crawls across the sky, tying together horizons to bind a day, calling it good and complete. It carries out its daily commute, and the shadows bend and bow. One morning the blue harebell does not rise, but the Indian blanket blooms in its place, splashing the meadow in flaming yellow, orange, and red; the kind of fire we welcome here in the forest. The sun picks off days, and the meadow yields and obeys.

"We are but of yesterday and know nothing." We forget the sun's many passages that brought us to where we are. We cannot recall the lessons and life held in tightly wrapped flower buds, waiting to unfurl. Then at once, they unfold, stretch out their petals, and unpack their wisdom. Just as quickly, they weaken, wilt, and fall at the tease of time. If we are not watching, we'll miss it. But we can be parents who watch and see, who set down our devices, look our children in their eyes, venture outside, and anchor time in nature-laced memories.

## How Do We Value Time?

Consider God looking down over your birth.

Stretched out before you is your life. You do not know the number of days you are given, but he does. He knows the years, months, weeks, days, hours, minutes, and seconds.

Now imagine him looking down over your life when it is half-spent. Is he or will he be pleased with how you are spending the time he has given you?

I imagine all of us feel that twinge of guilt or regret in our chests. None of us knows how best to spend our time. But I believe we innately know how *not* to spend it. God's Spirit is not shy in nudging us when we give our time to worthless things. The problem is we grow numb to that nudge.

What if you were to become greedy over your time? I don't mean spending it only for yourself—that is not at all biblical or wise. I mean this: You can refuse to let society and distractions steal your time. You can prayerfully decide how you want to spend your life and actually spend it that way. As you do, your children will live a secondhand intentional life. They will see your efforts in refusing to rush, denying distractions, and living life as the gift that it is.

In the opening chapter of this book, I mentioned that you don't need to move to the mountains to live a nature-full life. I hold to that. But at this point, I also want to share with you my family's catalyst, what finally severed the "mid" from our "west" and drove us to the Rocky Mountains.

It was the not-quite-spring of 2015, and my stomach was swollen with our third son. Our two boys were with my parents as Grayson and I snuck in a "babymoon" trip before a new baby would join our family. Driving through the Ozark Mountains, fog licked at the summits, and rain pelted on the windshield. Besides getting coffee, we had no plan. We spent the morning cruising through foothills, wading through the river, exploring backroads, and—unbeknownst to us—overhauling our life.

I unwound my leather journal and opened to a blank page. At the top, I wrote, "Family Values." We began creating a blueprint for our family. The first page was a brain dump, anything and everything that felt important to us.

"Exploration," we wrote. And with it: adventure, awe, wonder, respect, creativity, and travel.

We wanted our kids to hear the gospel in our home. To make conversations around faith normal and comfortable, an ebb and flow of our daily dialogue.

We wanted them to see God.

We wrote about education and hands-on learning; of decision-making and problem-solving and physical activity.

It was rough around the edges, but it was a start, and that was all we needed. Because looking up from that list at our current life, we recognized an alarming chasm. We were not living the life we wanted.

That little list would be a key in the ignition to another long day in the car, six months later with all three of our boys crammed into the back seat. This time we headed to a different mountain range: the Rocky Mountains of Colorado. We were pursuing a couple of the items we had written months before on our Family Values list: exploration and adventure.

Over the next ten days, not only would we be hiking and exploring. We would also be dropping off résumés, scoping out the housing market, and finding local playgrounds and coffee shops that we could soon call our own.

The list we'd written wasn't a wish list. It was a "how we need to do life" list. It was a list of all of the things we would regret in twenty years if we did not make them a priority right away. I recognized in nature a unique connection with God. Out on the trails and surrounded by creation, I felt nearer to him. We wanted that for our family.

Have you felt a similar pull? What could it look like to begin heeding those internal nudges and making them a reality for your family? In nature, we can discover a slower and more purposeful way of life. Perceiving the cadence of creation, I believe we, too, can slow down. We can collaborate with time. We can go outside and make it so much fuller.

Our Family Values list was a response to Ephesians 5:15–16, which warns, "Look carefully then how you walk, not as unwise but as wise, making the best use of the time, because the days are evil."

Living by default, our days lean toward evil; they are given to decay and waste. *Walk carefully.*

That day as my family wandered through the woods, I grabbed my daughter's hand—her other still clinging to the thick stem of the sugarbowl flower—and we waded through endless pine.

Time doesn't exist here.

Or maybe, this is where time is made.

## *Step Outside*

None of us knows the number of our days—only that they are limited. Challenge yourself to begin thinking about time differently, as a valuable resource and gift from God. Shorter even than our lives are our kids' childhoods. By making small, intentional shifts in how we spend our time and giving more of it to outdoor adventures, we can live wisely and teach our children to do the same.

Are there certain things you want for your family that you haven't made time for? Begin now by writing a list. It doesn't have to be neat or organized. Simply write down everything you feel is important for your family, then consider how to start prioritizing those things and making them a reality in your family's story. You can download a free step-by-step Family Values Guide on my website at www.eryn lynum.com/values.

## See Nature in the Bible

- Read to your children the verses below and ask them the following questions about time:
  - » "Teach us how short our lives really are so that we may be wise" (Psalm 90:12 NCV). Did you know that time is a gift from God? What do you think are some wise or smart ways to use the time God gives us?
  - » "So be very careful how you live. Do not live like those who are not wise, but live wisely. Use every chance you have for doing good, because these are evil times" (Ephesians 5:15–16 NCV). What are some ways we can be very careful in how we live? How can we protect our time? How can we use our time to do good?
- Read to your children Psalm 139:16–17 (NCV): "You saw my body as it was formed. All the days planned for me were written in your book before I was one day old. God, your thoughts are precious to me. They are so many!" Share with them how our lives are like stories, and God is the writer of our stories. He writes great adventures, and when we use our time and live life as he wants us to, we get to live out his amazing plans and enjoy life to its fullest!

## See God in Nature

Write into your calendar a day in the next month to devote entirely to outdoor play. Be flexible with the weather, even if you have to simply wait for a beautiful day and cancel what was previously planned. Pack plenty of snacks and books, and perhaps a few helpful tools like a magnifying glass, binoculars, nature reference books, and a notebook. Pack camp chairs or a picnic blanket. Find a natural area with opportunities for exploration and play. Here are some ideas:

- A green space with trees to climb
- A shallow creek
- A beach with at least one shady spot (or bring an umbrella)
- A wooded area
- A nature trail with a spot to sit and set up your picnic spot
- A paved trail that winds through several natural areas to explore throughout the day

Don't have anything else on the calendar that day or any need to return home. Let the entire goal be to lose your sense of time. Embrace boredom, allow your children to create their own games, and enjoy a good book on a beautiful day. Your children will probably achieve the goal of forgetting time much sooner than you do. Follow their lead. To encourage them in thinking about God's activities in nature, throughout the day casually work in questions such as:

- Why do you think God chose these colors for this flower?
- Why do you think God gave different birds different songs?
- When Jesus was on Earth, do you think he enjoyed nature?
- If God had given you the job of naming animals, what would you have named squirrels (or chipmunks, turtles, birds—whatever you see)?

— *10* —

# Family Hibernation

*Late lies the wintry sun a-bed,*
*A frosty, fiery sleepy-head;*
*Blinks but an hour or two; and then,*
*A blood-red orange, sets again.*
ROBERT LOUIS STEVENSON

HAVE YOU EVER TASTED A sweet cherry tomato straight from the vine in summer? What about a crisp apple from a tree at the height of autumn? There are wonderful benefits—both in flavor and health— to eating seasonally. But what about *resting* seasonally? I was thinking about this one predawn morning as the moon put on a grand display.

I had never seen the moon set—not like this: full, impossibly bright, and etched in intricate detail.

"It will go behind the mountains any minute," my husband commented, joining me at the table with a mug of hot coffee in his hands.

The sun waited its turn, brimming at the opposite horizon. Our piece of the world was still dark, except for the moon. A black canopy shrouded the mountains. We could not make out where mountain summits eclipse the skyline until . . . My husband was right; the moon's circumference was sliced by darkness.

This next part took only minutes. The moon swiftly tucked itself behind the peaks. Relative to something as still as the mountains, the moon's pace—or rather, the earth's rotation—felt dizzyingly quick. Yet time held, along with my breath.

As its final slice of yellow orb slipped behind the hills, the moon disappeared entirely. A moonset is much different than a sunset. When the sun obscures itself behind the mountains, brilliant rays and colors play across the sky as an epilogue. It is as if the sun stretches its luminous fingers across the horizon, grasping each final wisp of day. The moon, on the other hand, is tired and willing. With no light of its own to trail the sky, it simply relents. It knows its time.

Over the next few mornings, I woke to see if I could catch this phenomenon again, but the moon has an agenda. Now the sun lit the sky before the moon had a chance to hide behind the mountains. It seemed our moonset was a rarity. A gift.

I'm becoming familiar with the rhythms of the sun and moon. Every sunrise and sunset, along with the moon's journey across the night sky, remind me of my place in time. They challenge me to a slower way of life. We can invite creation's rhythms to set our pace, to remind us there are limits to a day.

In *The Ruthless Elimination of Hurry*, John Mark Comer lays out an insightful timeline of, well, time—specifically humanity's relationship with it and how that relationship shifted with technological advancements. Comer writes about history before the 1300s: "Time was natural. It was linked to the rotation of the earth on its axis and the four seasons. You went to bed with the moon and got up with the sun. Days were long and busy in summer, short and slow in winter. There was a rhythm to the day and even the year."[1] Comer continues, "When the sun set our rhythms of work and rest, it did so under the control of God."[2] He explains the impact of the sundial and the clock and how these albeit helpful contributions to society created a constraint on time, an awareness that can be beneficial but isn't always. He continues with Edison's invention of the light bulb in 1879, allowing people to stay up well past sundown.

Comer states that before the light bulb, people slept an average of eleven hours each night. Today, we're down to seven. How are we filling that extra four hours of awake time? You can give your family an advantage by harnessing "extra" hours and creating a calm culture in your home. This is what nature models for us. Looking at creation, we can heed lessons from hibernating creatures and recognize the gifts of respite and refreshment that God has tucked into the seasons. We can adopt a more natural pace and step into a rhythm of rest.

## "The Sleeping One"

We all have this ache for rest embedded into our souls, it is a design from our Creator, the One who knows we'll work ourselves raw if he doesn't intervene.

The morning we caught the moonset happened to take place during our family's annual winter hibernation. It is a practice we began six years ago, at first as a reaction. We had let screen time slip out of hand. The TV had to go.

My husband proposed an intriguing idea: "Why don't we hibernate?"

At his simple suggestion, our motive flip-flopped. It was no longer about restriction or what we were losing (the TV); it was about gain: eternal and soul-feeding gain.

In taking a break from TV, reining in screen time, and saying no to work in the evenings, we opened up new margins for beauty, inspiration, and rest. Out came game boards, novels, and candles.

Hibernating during dark, cold winters is something that has taken place for thousands of years as an opportunity for the land to rest. Animals hibernate out of a scarcity of food. When provisions and resources are slim in cold months, animals go into a lingering sleepy state. They awaken to spring's thaw when food buds, blossoms, and buzzes back.

A peculiar bird, the common poorwill, offers us an intriguing example of hibernation. In the winter months, when food is hard to find, most birds migrate to warmer climates. The ones that don't move, known as resident birds, live off plants, seeds, and dried berries. Other birds that rely on insects for their meals hit the skies. A busy season of migration ensues. We don't see much of it because birds often make their migratory flights at night, but the skies are a flurry of activity as billions of birds react to cooling temperatures.

But not the common poorwill. He *should* take an extended vacation to where there are plenty of insects to eat. Instead, he hangs back with the resident birds. How the common poorwill survives the winter is fascinating. He is the only known bird to hibernate. Long before scientists discovered the poorwill's capacity to hibernate, the Hopi Native American tribe must have known. Their name for the poorwill means "the sleeping one."

We can all take a lesson from the common poorwill. When the pace of life speeds up and society around us is all abuzz, we can hibernate by simplifying our agendas, curbing our spending, limiting our consumption, and hunkering down with a great book and a cozy candle.

## Hibernation Triggers

We may not find ourselves lacking food in winter, with holiday feasts and treats. But we suffer from a completely different scarcity: rest, peace, and calm. In animals, depleted food sources aren't the only thing that tell them it's time to hunker down and hibernate. It is believed that they also have a compound in their blood known as

Hibernation Induction Trigger (HIT), although how exactly this compound works remains a bit of a mystery to scientists.

Maybe we, too, have specific triggers that tell us when it's time to rest. Ours could look more like increased illness, irritability, sleeplessness, anxiety, fatigue, burned-out adrenal glands, lack of focus, loss of joy, anger . . . The list goes on. Maybe like with Hibernation Induction Triggers in an animal, God uses these signals to tell us when rest is no longer an avoided option but essential to our survival.

Our annual two-week practice of hibernation acts as a radical reset for my family's schedule and souls as we step into a sacred time of rest. Like a bear hunkering down in its den to wait out the chill of winter, my family has come to eagerly embrace this time of calm, cozy evenings after busy holidays. It is a readjustment of our pace in life. But what does it actually look like?

## How to Hibernate As a Family

"But what about work?" One mama asked me after a speaking event. The topic of screen time detox was bouncing around the room. The idea of hibernation piqued the audience's interest.

"Don't get me wrong; we work," I explained. "Hibernation is not the same as a staycation. Work, school, cleaning, tantrums, discipline, sibling quarrels—all of these still take place. But in the midst of it, a rhythm of rest keeps us upright and centered."

In becoming a collector of sunsets and sunrises (and recently moonsets!), I've found that a circadian rhythm has begun to reset my soul to a healthier relationship with time. A recent sunrise over our ice-coated lake was no exception. Sitting at our dining room table, hoping to steal an hour of work before my kids woke, I saw colors dance across the sky, beckoning me to stop and watch.

Sunrises don't wait. They don't "hold on a minute" while we finish a task. I wonder how true this is of my children as well. How many times have I told them to "wait an (arbitrary) minute" as I finish something up before coming to see what they're pining to show me? How much fleeting beauty have I traded for my pursuit of productivity?

Creation's natural rhythms, guided by the sun and moon, act as patterns for hibernation. While many of our daily activities remain the same, evening takes on a new tone. The sun's setting is a cue to put away work, light candles, play calm music, and reach for a good book or a board game.

Hibernation can and should (and will) look different from home to home. If a parent works evening shifts, a family might need to focus on slow mornings for hibernation. Some years our hibernation has happened in December, other years in January or February, depending on my husband's work projects. The first year will most likely include some hesitation and rebuttal. But please believe me that this practice will have an eternal impact on your family. One of the sweetest gifts hibernation has given us is its stubborn refusal to remain within the two rows we allot it on the calendar. Year by year, it has seeped out of those boundaries and begun to change the entire culture of our home throughout the year. Eight years in, we don't even mark it on the calendar. Instead, we simply find as the days grow shorter, we ease into hibernation. We lean toward rest.

Whatever your hibernation looks like, here are some helpful focus points.

### Set Screen-Free Evenings

Let me preface this: hibernation does include a couple of family movie nights. It's fun to set a theme, maybe watch a couple of classics, musicals, or old-time favorites.

As you practice hibernation for the first time and begin limiting screens, there might be a hefty dose of pushback. As I mentioned, this yearly ritual began as a reaction. Screen time was taking over our home and our kids' attitudes. But every year has become easier. Let your kids fall in love with the nostalgia of game nights and read alouds, and eagerly anticipate an extended season of rest each year.

### Welcome Calm and Quiet

This is a time to stream instrumental music from a speaker and set a cadence in the evenings. Light candles, cozy up, and settle in for a drawn-out time of togetherness.

As you lower the lights, an ambiance will settle over your home. Your kids might initially feel a need to dance and run and play in the darkness—that's ok! Hibernation is meant to be fun. But then let them migrate to a stack of books or a table with art supplies. Although hibernation is never perfect, it can day-by-day and year-by-year change the culture of your home and the pace of your family.

### Family Time

Preparation for hibernation normally includes a trip to the library, where we all stock up on good reads. Books are strewn about the house, ready to fill hands, minds, and hearts. I'm a firm believer that a good book should always be within arm's reach. As we read together (or separately, but side by side), the stories accumulate into a narrative of hibernation. We give time to watercolors, activity books, sketching, coloring, and games. With screens put away, our evenings are free to fill with creative and inspiring endeavors. On the weekends, hibernation also includes family hikes or walks or trips to the library. On a recent hibernating morning, nearly a foot of fresh snow welcomed us outside. For over an hour, we walked the neighborhood, sledded, and played together as a family before returning inside to warm drinks and good books.

*Together-Focused Outings*

In the spirit of family time, you can also plan a couple of low-key outings. These do *not* include busy shopping centers, big events, traffic, or running errands. They might include:

- Sledding hills
- Ice-skating
- Winter hiking
- Bird-watching
- Drives through the countryside

This year brought my favorite hibernation outing yet. We packed the SUV full of kids (just ours, we have a lot), winter gear, sleds, and shovels and drove one and a half hours to an area we knew had a lot of snowfall. Hoarfrost clung to every pine branch as if the frozen crystals had budded from the tree itself. Only a few brave skiers were at our spot when we arrived. We spent over two hours climbing through hip-deep snow, sledding, sitting around a fire in the middle of a pine forest, all while perfect snow flurries fell over the woods.

Hibernation is a perfect opportunity to create outdoor memories your family will harbor in their hearts forever.

*Protect Quiet Evenings*

During these two weeks, we try our best to limit activities that take us apart. We don't do this perfectly, mind you, but we're much more aware of what we give our time to outside the home. Hibernation is a time to protect your quiet evenings together.

You can also invite others in to experience the gift of intentional rest. As I've surrendered unrealistic expectations of a perfect house and learned to order pizza rather than preparing an impressive meal, we've had more get-togethers under our roof during hibernation. It has become a sweet time of welcoming others into the coziness of the season.

Eight years into this, I can observe how the practice of hunkering down during winter has changed our family as a whole. As you practice circling back to rest, the circle will become smaller and the path shorter. You will have less distance to return, less to reset, and fewer distractions to bushwhack through because you'll find yourself always near our Father's heart of rest.

## The Spirit Behind Rest

After creating the world, God rested not because he needed to but because there was much to delight in. God understands the value of Sabbath, of "stopping and delighting" in work that's been accomplished.

In Genesis 2:2–3 we read: "He rested on the seventh day from all his work that he had done. So God blessed the seventh day and made it holy, because on it God rested from all his work that he had done in creation." We have to wonder what that first day of rest looked like. Although most of us, with a day void of activity, would opt for a nap, that's not how God spent his day off, as Psalm 121:3–4 tells us God does not sleep. Instead, imagine him like a child in a meadow. Maybe he listened thoughtfully—or thoughtlessly—to every bird he'd placed in the sky, taking in each unique song. Maybe he studied the new colors he'd conjured up, displayed in a stretching carpet of wildflowers. Perhaps he strode along a river, counting the brilliantly colored fish as frogs jumped from the bank into the chilly waters. Maybe he stared up into the sky and considered which clouds reflected what shapes he'd created all week.

What if we had a similar rapt attention? It is something we can develop through restful time in nature. Aligning our lives with creation's pace, our souls can come to a full stop and take delight in all God has made.

## Step Outside

In nature we find a rhythm of intentional rest. Creation invites us to live within the boundaries God set for our health and wellness. You get to choose how fast or how slow your family lives life. But if you're not protective of your time, others will choose how you spend it. They'll assign their agendas to your family's story. Living in tune with God's timing and seasons helps us recognize these dangers and choose a different way.

Hibernation is a life-giving practice in intentional rest. By setting aside this special time, your family can break away from distractions and reconvene around what's important. You can live for what you value and pass those values along to your children all while living at a sustainable pace that fosters play, wonder, and rest.

### See Nature in the Bible

- Read to your children Genesis 2:1–3 and use the following questions and discussion points:
  - » Why do you think God rested? Was he tired? (Read Isaiah 40:28, which states that God does not grow weary.)
  - » Many people call this day of rest *Shabbat* or *Sabbath*. It means "to stop and delight." God rested as an example for us. He wants us to rest and enjoy life. How can we practice stopping our work and delighting in all God has made?
- Whether or not you practice a regular Sabbath rest, choose one day in the coming month to put all work away and rest as a family. Read Hebrews 4:9–10 and decide together how to enjoy a day of rest and delight. Consider going on a family walk or bike ride, playing outside, or having a picnic dinner.

### See God in Nature

After exploring God's heart for rest in the above section "See Nature in the Bible," take a walk outside and discuss how nature rests. Here are some examples you can talk about:

- In the springtime, parent birds work all day long to gather food and feed their young. They have to sleep very well to have energy for the next day.
- Hummingbirds flap their wings so rapidly that they have to practice a mini "hibernation" called "torpor" every night. They sleep so deeply that their heart rate slows way down.
- Some plants grow back every year. They are known as perennials. They rest their roots during wintertime so they can grow back stronger each spring.
- Trees shed their leaves every fall so that they can rest throughout winter. Since they don't need to "feed" their growing leaves, they can survive cold months.
- Bears don't actually hibernate. Instead, they go into a long, sleepy nap where they wake occasionally throughout the winter months. Mama bears give birth during this time. Their long nap gives them the energy they need to feed and protect their cubs.
- Ask your children if they see any other examples of rest in nature. Looking at creation, do they think God finds rest important?

# — 11 —

# Creation and Creativity

*I like nature because it works well.*
WILL LYNUM, AGE 4

HAVE YOU EVER HAD A creative block or struggled to encourage your children in their creativity? In a society where we're often being told what to think, or pacified with entertainment, it's difficult to break back into our God-given creativity. Yet God gave us nature as the ultimate source of creative inspiration. We can see it as our kids play outdoors. They are naturally inclined to create things with nature's materials. As we encourage them in this endeavor, their ingenuity, problem-solving, and sense of beauty develop. One of my favorite examples of a human-made design modeled after God's art is found in a bright blue bird with a mohawk—or "crest"—that lives along the riverways.

On a cold January afternoon, I stopped mid-run along a riverside path to watch my favorite bird. Its sharp features, piercing beak, and sleek shape gave it away. The belted kingfisher perched on a cotton-wood branch overhanging the water. I have witnessed on other days the exquisite fishing display of kingfishers along the river. They glide through the air parallel to the water below, swooping up at the last minute to land on a cottonwood branch. They swoop back and forth, scanning the water below and calling in their telltale clicking song. Once a fish is spotted, the bird dives with exceptional speed and accuracy to catch its meal.

It is this bird's impressive dive that solved a massive problem for Japanese engineers in the late 1990s. One of the planet's busiest high-speed rail lines was developed in Japan in 1964. The rail line, Tokaido Shinkansen, moved billions of passengers throughout the country. Yet there was a problem. Traveling through a tunnel at speeds of 150–200 miles per hour, the train built up atmospheric pressure at its nose. Emerging from the tunnel, this pressure would explode into a "tunnel sonic boom," waking babies from naps, disturbing focused businesspeople, disrupting school days, and altogether serving as a constant and loud interruption to daily life. The exploding noise could be heard nearly a quarter mile from the tunnel.

Asked to invent a newer, faster, yet quieter train, a team of engineers set to work, but not exactly with machines and materials. Instead, they first looked to nature. Considering the problem at hand, they dissected the issue down to its core: a sudden change in air resistance. Eiji Nakatsu, the general engineer in charge of the bullet train's technical development, proposed this solution: "Is there some living thing that manages sudden changes in air resistance as a part of daily life? Yes, there is, the kingfisher."[1]

When faced with a challenge, it wasn't his background in engineering that Nakatsu tapped into. Instead, it was his experience as an avid bird-watcher and active member of the Wild Bird Society of Japan. He must have been familiar with the bird's ability to dive into the water at twenty-five miles per hour without making so much as a splash.

Inspired by the kingfisher's shape and aerodynamics, Nakatsu's team designed an entirely new bullet train. In 1997, the Shinkansen bullet train was put into commercial use. It proved faster, quieter, and more energy efficient than prior models. The nose of the train directly resembles the shape of a kingfisher's beak.

What answers to life's questions can our children discover as they learn to peer intently into God's designs?

## Becoming Apprentices to the Maker

Each time I watch a kingfisher strategically hover over its target and gracefully dive for the catch, I'm reminded of what my youngest son once told me on a hike.

"I like nature," he told me, "because it works well." He sees beyond the face value of beauty (albeit a wonderful facet of creation) and deeper into the architecture, design, and engineering of everything around us. Have you seen this attention to detail in your children? At times it might need to be retrained, yet all that requires is time outdoors without an agenda. When our kids are surrounded by beautiful things, they engage, dissect, construct, and create. As they do, they realize rhyme and reason in the materials they're working with.

*It works well*, my son told me. Perhaps that's why, in the field of biomimetics, designers, engineers, and architects have long sought answers to problems from existing models found in nature.

Along with a high-speed train mimicking the aerodynamics of a kingfisher's beak, we find numerous other human inventions drawing lines straight back to nature.

A gecko's sticky feet, created for climbing, contributed insight for adhesives.

Wind turbine blades are modeled after the arc and curve of a humpback whale's fin.

After plucking spiny burrs from his dog's fur, Swiss engineer George de Mestral studied the spiny seed and from it invented Velcro.

A shopping center in Zimbabwe is modeled after the ingenious ventilation design termites use in their mounds.

Have you ever watched (with shivers up your spine) a spider maneuvering tight spaces? A robot prototype is currently in design to mimic a spider's agile movements to navigate and locate survivors amid rubble after natural disasters.

In *Science and the Mind of the Maker*, Melissa Cain Travis explains, "The fields of scientific research and engineering that look to biological designs for the invention and improvement of human technology are called *biomimetics* and *bioinspiration*."[2] Cain goes on to explain the differences. Biomimetics directly copies designs in nature. Bioinspiration takes inspiration from nature and applies it to solve non-biological problems. Simply put: scientists and engineers (we could include architects, artists, and anyone who creates anything) blatantly copy, or at least draw inspiration from, nature's designs. It is exactly what I'm doing in this book. God's creation and designs influence every page. This is the "steal like an artist" concept.

In his *New York Times* best-selling book *Steal Like an Artist*, author Austin Kleon proposes that all creative endeavors are, to varying extents, copies of other art. Everything we create has a flavor of something already made. Kleon clarifies that by *steal*, he does not mean rip-off or plagiarize. He refers to a profound act of studying, admiring, learning from, and finding inspiration in the work of others. When we "steal" from the designs in nature, we acknowledge the beauty and mastery evident throughout creation and extend its reach and impact through our work. Kleon explains that we copy our heroes, those whose work we greatly admire. He wrote, "The reason you copy your heroes and their style is so that you might somehow get a glimpse into their minds."[3]

Drawing inspiration from creation and allowing it to guide our work, we better understand the Creator's mind. Melissa Cain Travis further explains on the topic of biomimetics, "Perhaps we could say that human engineers working in biomimetics and bioinspiration are, practically speaking, apprentices to the Maker."[4]

We can help our kids become apprentices to the Maker. We can allow them to spend copious amounts of time surrounded by the most inspiring scenes, ideas, concepts, and materials this planet offers. Through every exposure to nature, they can sit at the feet of their Maker and learn from his ways, wonder, and wisdom.

Recently, my children sat in swiveling chairs around our library's 3D printer, eagerly hanging onto the technician's every word. They watched the introductory film on how to use the printer, learning where to locate models, how to upload them to the software, and what to do (and not do) as they patiently wait for their designs to print. After signing paperwork, my kids became certified to use the machine.

"I will be in that other room if you have any questions or want help with anything," the technician assured us. Then he left my children—and me as a grossly unqualified 3D printer chaperone—to our creativity.

My oldest son opened an internet browser on the screen and typed in the URL on our information sheet for where to search for existing models. The screen revealed endless designs sitting at his fingertips that he could pull into three-dimensional form. He could have chosen anything. Lego bricks for his collection, a tool for his treehouse building, a container to hold coins, a character from a movie. Instead, he set his fingers to the keys and typed, "Bird."

Over the next hour and thirteen minutes, we watched careful, precise layers form a three-inch tall avian friend. It was a new category of bird-watching for us. When it came time to create, my son's experiences in nature acted as his guide as he engineered a bird.

John Muir, the late naturalist and mountaineer, was also an engineer. He was said to have left his career in mechanical inventions to study instead "the inventions of God."[5] A devastating accident nearly cost him the sight in his eye. John Muir thought his eye was "closed forever on all God's beauty."[6] With the care of a specialist eye doctor, Muir recovered his sight and, with it, a newfound eagerness to see all God has made. He quickly made his way to the woods. Upon stepping out of the dark room where he'd spent several months recovering, Muir wrote:

> As soon as I got out into Heaven's light I started on another long excursion, making haste with all my heart to store my mind with the Lord's beauty and thus be ready for any fate, light or dark. And it was from this time that my long continuous wanderings may be said to have fairly commenced. I bade adieu to all my mechanical inventions, determined to devote the rest of my life to the study of the inventions of God.[7]

Have you ever found similar inspiration in nature? Have you spent time in God's creation and discovered the answer to a question on your mind or a solution to a problem you are facing? Sometimes God uses the light of nature to draw us out from the darkness of circumstances. As he does, we are given new perspective and inspiration. This is a journey we can help our children take. In allowing them time to explore God's designs, we introduce them to the One who will meet their needs, answer their questions, and inspire them in all their creative endeavors.

## God Practiced Restraint in Nature

Do you believe God reins in his power and that he practices restraint? In nature, we find examples of both, and these models of self-control point us and our kids to a God who is strategic and mindful in all he does.

In *Natural Theology*, William Paley poses this idea behind God's inspiring designs: "Whatever is done, God could have done without the intervention of instruments or means: but it is in the construction of instruments, in the choice and adaption of means, that a creative intelligence is seen. It is this which constitutes the order and beauty of the universe. God, therefore, has been pleased to prescribe limits to his own power, and to work his end within those limits."[8]

This idea of God limiting himself chafed against my theological understanding. It begs the mind-twisting question, "If God can do anything, can he limit what he does?"

I wrestled with this question until I realized this reining in of power is not about what he *can* do but about what he *will* do. He introduced needs in nature so we would have the opportunity to see the need-meeter. As he spoke everything into place in the beginning, he could have made the plants of the earth capable of watering themselves. He could have made our bodies reenergize themselves, nullifying dependency on food. He could have met every need in creation forever. Instead, as a God of order, he chose to design systems and strategies. He engineered the universe to support every living thing he had made, including us. In those designs, we gain a glimpse into the mind of our Maker.

And so, his construction of designs was an act of restraint. Isaiah 55:8–9 tells us:

> For my thoughts are not your thoughts,
>     neither are your ways my ways, declares the LORD.
> For as the heavens are higher than the earth,
>     so are my ways higher than your ways
>     and my thoughts than your thoughts.

His ways are beyond our comprehension, yet he reins them in and confines them to systems we can explore, research, peer into, and understand.

Consider for a moment if he had not practiced restraint. If God spoke nature into place using language and means entirely outside the scope of our understanding, would we ever see hints of an intelligent mind? Instead, by carefully choosing means and methods within our brains' reach, he left notes to pique our interest. He invited us to explore and discover him as our Maker. Perhaps God created needs within nature so we could see exactly how he meets those needs so that one day we'd give him a chance to meet our own.

## Nature Is the Greatest Classroom

Put simply, nature is wildly inspiring and is most often the greatest classroom. When we consider the life of Christ and his three years in active ministry, we realize he spent a significant amount of time teaching. Countless hours were invested in his disciples, presenting sermons to crowds, and giving impromptu lessons to those who crossed his path. Where did Christ most often teach? In the great outdoors.

In his book *The Man Nobody Knows*, Bruce Barton shined a light on an often-overlooked characteristic of Jesus. In highlighting Jesus as an outdoorsman, Barton wrote:

> All his days were spent in the open air . . . the greater part of his teaching was done on the shores of his lake, or in the cool recesses of the hills. He walked constantly from village to village; his face was tanned by the sun and wind. Even at night he slept outdoors, when He could—turning his back on the hot walls of the city and slipping away into the healthful freshness of the Mount of Olives.[9]

I believe Jesus found his inspiration and taught lessons in the open air because he wanted to be surrounded by everything he and his father had fashioned together at creation. I have no doubt there was a sense of nostalgia whenever Jesus dipped his toes into a lake, walked along a riverbank, or sat among a grove of trees.

"In the beginning was the Word," John 1:1–4 tells us, "and the Word was with God, and the Word was God. He was in the beginning with God. All things were made through him, and without him was not any thing made that was made. In him was life, and the life was the light of men."

The Word, here, refers directly to Jesus Christ. Present at creation, Jesus shared an intimate connection to and familiarity with every aspect of the natural world. Time and again, he used specific details in nature to prove points about God, humanity, and humanity's relationship to God.

Following Jesus's example, we can utilize nature's materials to guide our children into a deeper understanding of who God is and how he loves us.

## Creating from Creation

Have you ever watched your children create something—whether through paint, crayons, clay, words on paper, a skit or song, or any other materials—that directly reflected God's creation? Through creating, our children experience a unique connection to their Creator.

I saw this on an afternoon in March as my family played at the river. Most of the surface remained frozen, but some water had broken through thinner ice sheets. The river flowed up and over the ice, then back into another hole. No one was calling this spring yet, except the fly-fishers standing out where the water was free. They understand long before most of us do when spring has arrived. It's not in the obvious arrival of wildflowers. Instead, spring arrives first at the river.

The macroinvertebrate insects had hatched, and both the fish and birds knew it. Trout ran wild in the waters. A pair of sleek black American dippers flew, swooped, dove, and came up with caddisfly hatchlings.

I watched a dipper take his still-shelled catch over to a large rock. He skillfully whacked the insect against the rock until the fleshy inside broke loose from its shell. The bird swallowed it whole then scanned the water for another.

I turned to our third son, who was busy on the shore with his watercolor set. I walked over and bent down to see his canvas. It mirrored the dark gray rock cliff across the water, the river flowing gracefully around it, and the sun sitting high in the afternoon sky.

I didn't know he could paint like that.

Regrettably, we did not let him finish. It was time to leave. "I'm going to remember the river," he told me as he packed up his supplies, "so I can finish this when we get home." To my amazement, he did, and it was a masterpiece.

Nature gently lifts us out of a creative rut. It provides formulas and solutions for complex problems. It answers our questions, then asks us better ones. Pulling inspiration from nature, we're taking from God's ingenuity and creativity.

In Genesis, when we read about something being created or made, there are two Hebrew words: *bārā'* (baw-raw) and *'āśâ* (aw-saw). While the latter, *'āśâ*, can be used interchangeably whether it is God or a human making something, *bārā'* is different; it always refers to God as the Creator. We see it in the very first verse of the Bible: "In the beginning, God created [*bārā'*] the heavens and the earth." It often implies something being made from nothing, like in Hebrews 11:3, "By faith we understand that the universe was created by the word of God, so that what is seen was not made out of things that are visible."

When we humans make something, we always ʿāśâ, or make something from existing elements. That afternoon along the river, my son created a stunning watercolor painting inspired by shapes, colors, dimensions, depths, lighting, and shadows already in existence. He used elements spoken into place long ago at creation.

The word *ʿāśâ* is our calling. We share what God has made and who he is through the materials he has already given us. We create from existing materials, while God created everything without prior design. There were no blueprints, color palettes, or texture samples, and he had zero external creative inspiration to draw from. Yet during creation, God spoke into existence all the creative potential we would ever need. Math, science, shapes, cause and effect, colors, dimensions, and patterns—God created the potential for all our future creative endeavors, as well as answers to complex issues. Author John Mark Comer writes, "To be made in the image of God means that we're rife with potential. We have the Divine's capacity in our DNA. We're *like* God. We were created to image His behavior, to *rule* like He does, to gather up the raw materials of our planet and reshape them into a world for human beings to flourish and thrive."[10]

Your children are rife with potential. We can see this practice of creatively reflecting God carried out by our children nearly every time we go outside. Their hands are eager for the earth's raw materials. Surrounded by nature, they have no lack of inspiration. They will look for problems to conquer: a tree branch just out of reach, a stream too wide to cross on foot, a foreboding rain cloud and no shelter, a snowy field with no fallout shelter or shield from impending snowballs. They have a throbbing need inside them to solve these problems. Quickly they begin hatching plans and gathering materials from their surroundings.

Perhaps God supplied patterns for our lives in the reasonableness and rationale of nature. And maybe as we and our kids spend more time out of doors, our own lives will make more sense. Problems will settle into solutions. Or maybe in the perspective of everything lovely and true, the problems just won't matter as much anymore.

## God's Designs Work Best

As our children witness and come into a deeper understanding of God's detailed designs and how well his inventions work, I believe they will have more stability in an ever-shifting society.

One morning I was rushing to get myself and the kids ready to leave the house when my ten-year-old son came into my bathroom. I nearly brushed him off, telling him that he needed to go get his shoes on, but something told me to listen.

He asked, "Why did God make men and women different from each other? Why didn't he just make men, and men would marry men?"

As soon as he asked about male and female differences, I knew that he wasn't asking about homosexuality; that, I'm sure, will be for another day. Instead, his question was more straightforward: Why did God make variety? Why are men and women different from each other?

"Men's and women's bodies are like puzzle pieces," I explained. "The parts of their bodies fit together perfectly, and when they do, they can even make a baby. God made men to find women's bodies very attractive, so they see the shape of a woman and think, 'Wow, that is beautiful!' And for women to look at men and think, 'Wow, I like that!' God's design is for a man and a woman from different families to come together in a promise, and to only join their bodies together to each other."

I wondered if I was stumbling over my words and if I was saying too much, but then again, he's ten. He needs to understand these things, and I want to be the one walking him through these discussions.

"What about divorce?" he asked.

I marveled at his deep questions. This conversation was far more valuable than getting out of the house on time.

"Well, this world is broken. Sometimes things don't work very well, but God's grace is big enough for that. A man and a woman might marry, then divorce. Or a man might have sex with another woman, or the woman with another man, but it makes things very messy and hurtful. It doesn't work out well." I wanted him to see the chasm between God's designs and society's brokenness. As our kids begin to understand that God's plans for our lives are best, the world's offerings become less appealing. They can begin to see the enemy's lies for what they are and contrast them to God's promises and life-giving ways.

I went on to explain to my son, "God's design for family works best. Think about creation. Does creation work well? Think about the water cycle, ecosystems, and the moon guiding the seasons and the sun guiding the day. God's designs work very well! And we can trust his design for family works very well too."

The analogy made something click in his mind. He has stood at the headwaters of the Colorado River and seen the canyons and reservoir systems near our home. In school, he has studied the water cycle. He has witnessed the miracle of regrowth and restoration after wildfires. He understands the moon's pull on the ocean tides. The more he discovers nature's miraculous and meticulous designs, the more stable his faith becomes.

Our kids are asking countless questions as they attempt to piece together an understanding of the world. As they grow older, the questions become more complicated. Yet you can develop a sensitivity to stop and listen when they come to you with these inquiries. Every time we prioritize their questions, their trust in us deepens. By offering a listening ear and taking them out in nature where they see God at work, our kids can gain confidence in the One who makes all things good.

## *Step Outside*

Your children have creativity etched into their DNA. God creates us to create. When we make beautiful things, we experience a deep sense of purpose and fulfillment. Nature offers a wonderful invitation to practice our God-given ingenuity and make things that directly reflect his glory. As your children engage with nature's materials, they will discover reason and method behind all God has made. If your children are struggling with creativity, take them outside. Walk along a river or through the woods. Sit and watch birds in the trees. Lie on the ground and watch clouds crawl across the sky. Allow God's creativity to inspire your children, and watch in wonder as they take those designs and reinterpret them through their own creative endeavors.

### See Nature in the Bible

Read Psalm 104:5–24 in an easy-to-understand Bible translation like the New Century Version or the New Living Translation. If your children are able to, invite them to read parts of the passage. Ask what systems and designs God has made in nature, whether from the passage or from what they see outside. Some designs to draw from the passage are:

- Mountains rising to create canyons and riverways, bringing water from the mountaintops to the oceans
- Freshwater springs providing water for the earth
- Grass and plants growing as food for animals and people
- Birds created as master engineers to build incredible nest designs for their families
- The moon guiding seasons
- Daytime and nighttime

### See God in Nature

Referring to Psalm 104:5–24, invite your kids to use whatever art supplies they want to recreate one of God's designs. They can also incorporate natural materials such as sticks, pine cones, and fallen leaves. This is another activity that is best done with friends. Plan a few hours to visit a natural area. If it has picnic tables to work on, all the better. Bring an array of art supplies. If you're inviting friends, ask them to bring supplies as well. Here are some materials to consider:

- Paint (watercolor and acrylic)
- Crayons, markers, and colored pencils
- Oil pastel crayons
- Construction paper
- Glue and tape
- Hole puncher and scissors
- Popsicle sticks
- Colored string
- Pom-poms
- Pipe cleaners
- A garbage bag for cleanup
- A disposable tablecloth to keep the table clean

Invite the kids to share their art with each other afterward, talking about the details of what God has made and how it works well.

— 12 —

# Bringing Nature Indoors

*I firmly believe that nature brings*
*solace in all troubles.*

ANNE FRANK

You might be feeling some of the same tension or asking similar questions that I hear from readers of my blog or social media, or from parents I hear from at speaking events. How can you connect your children to God through nature if you live in an urban area or don't have access to natural landscapes?

Over thirteen years of marriage, my husband and I have lived in ten different homes. These range from a farmhouse on five acres, to a third-story apartment in a dangerous city, to a twenty-foot travel trailer parked at the ocean's edge, to our current home that sits on a lake. We have been rich and poor in our access to nature.

Yet what we have found is this: no matter where you are planted, you can create an atmosphere rich in God's wonders.

And sometimes, it begins inside.

A few years ago, when my joy began to flatline, I didn't see it as quickly as my husband did.

I felt it, of course, as negative emotions dragged my spirit down like an anchor. But I could not see how rapidly I was sinking.

"I mentioned it to the guys tonight," my husband, Grayson, told me after an evening with the men from our small group at church. "I told them I think you might have postpartum depression."

I was not offended that he told them. These families are our people. We need them. I was more shocked at the spoken term now hanging in the air between us. You can't suggest "postpartum depression" then sweep it back under the rug like it never happened. It felt foreign, yet it made sense. Our daughter was a few months old, and I was not myself.

Did it surprise me after a difficult pregnancy? Her not knowing me, me not knowing her, both of us stumbling together, trying to keep her alive inside my womb. After discovering irregular cardiac activity, the doctors prepared to take her out at thirty-three weeks.

But God having answered our prayers, my daughter stayed in my womb with her stubborn, erratic heart behavior for four more weeks. Then she arrived during a blizzard. The nurses placed her bare skin against my chest. Her five pounds felt like nothing—yet everything. Her hair was as white as the snow falling outside the window.

Bringing our newborn home, we were tired, as every parent is when they walk through the front door with a new child. But this was a compounded exhaustion. It was fatigue of both body and soul after nearly seven years of parenting. I was worn down from months of monitoring my little one's heart rate and counting kicks and praying for her life. I was weary from hospital visits several times a week, seeing specialists, and being admitted on several occasions for monitoring. All of it had left me sapped of energy.

And now, here she was, staring up into my eyes, expecting everything.

Deep affection stirred. I wanted to know her, my only daughter after three sons. But most of me felt hollow.

At four months, with her refusing to nurse, my hormones stirred like a rowdy, angry sea. I couldn't place them in straight order or compartmentalize the thoughts they roused. It was easier to turn inward. To shut down. To say I was just tired—and I was.

But now, my husband had spoken this term, *postpartum depression*, and we had to deal with it. It is not a term that sits around then carries itself off on a windy day, like a pile of leaves in autumn.

Now that he had said it, I could too. Awkwardly I spoke it to a room of close friends and asked them to pray. They agreed to cover me in prayer.

In the meantime, the great outdoors became my greatest medicine.

My daughter would nuzzle into me as I sat with her out in the sun. Or her brothers would scale heights at the playground as she and I lay in the shade and felt the blades of grass between our fingers and toes. We listened to the birds sing. We picked flowers. She was discovering. I was healing.

All the while, I was breaking. Yet it was like the necessary snapping when my boys hold a glow stick between their small hands. They carefully bend the plastic tubing until it cracks and light emerges. Have you ever felt God bending you and pressing you beyond your limits? He flexes our spirits, breaking old patterns until at last, light appears.

Somewhere amid this breaking and healing, I bought a houseplant. It stared at me from the grocery store shelf, this *Peperomia obtusifolia* or baby rubber plant. I brought it home.

That was the beginning of my obsession with bringing nature indoors.

The plant sat on the side table in our living room. I didn't know how to care for it, so I simply watered it when the soil was dry. By some miracle, it didn't die. But it did look lonely. So more plants quickly followed—not only live plants but freshly cut flowers as well.

The world outside began turning yellow and cold. Inside, we were greening. Plants filled corners, and flowers erupted from vases. My husband allowed it all. He must have seen something in my spirit shifting with all this life around.

The year following my daughter's birth was drenched in new life. Yes, it was a dark season, but only for a whisper of time. God delivered light and life, and our home—now always adorned in plants—is an aftereffect of that season. It's not only plants but tanks of live fish and bird feeders propped outside our windows. Rocks from our hikes and adventures line shelves and windowsills. Bird feathers stick out from soil in plant pots or between book pages. Nature is our decor.

Laura Ingalls once said, "It is the simple things of life that make living worthwhile, the sweet fundamental things such as love and duty, work and rest, and living close to nature."[1]

One way to live close to nature is to bring it indoors.

## Nature Makes Us Healthier and Happier

In general, would you say you feel healthier after experiencing God's creation? Have you felt physical, mental, emotional, or spiritual benefits from a walk along the river or through a park? Time with nature is a great advantage we can give our kids in every area of their health.

The mental and physical health benefits of being around nature are well documented, and they are even beginning to shape hospital designs. The science and health world grew curious about these findings in the wake of a study performed by Roger S. Ulrich, PhD, in 1984. Ulrich began researching the possible impact of nature exposure for patients' recovery. In his paper entitled *Health Benefits of Gardens in Hospitals*, Ulrich explained, "The discussion concentrates mainly on health-related benefits that patients realize by simply looking at gardens and plants, or in other ways passively experiencing healthcare surroundings where plants are prominent."[2]

It ends up, the prominence of plants makes a significant impact.

In observing post-surgery patients, Ulrich discovered that those with a view of nature were "in good spirits" and had shorter hospital stays, needed less narcotic pain medicine, and recovered better than those with a view of a brick wall out their window.[3] Plants make for healthier, happier patients. If a hospital is looking for positive online reviews from past customers, they might want to consider some potted ferns.

Historically winter has been heavy on my spirit. Living in Colorado has spoiled me with sunshine. If the skies bring us a succession of overcast days or temperatures too extreme to play outside, my mood declines. I'm not the greatest wife or mom in winter.

But something has been different the past couple of years. Two things, actually:

1. I adjusted my definition of "too cold to play outside." Acquiring proper winter gear, I have resolved to go outside each day, even if only for a few minutes.
2. When we're inside, nature is here too.

If you have ever walked through an indoor botanical garden or beneath the arches of glass aquarium walls teeming with life, you understand this effect. Experiencing nature indoors bridges a gap. It makes creation accessible all the time. Rhythms, songs, colors, and movements of the natural world create a new atmosphere for our inside spaces. Walking by a houseplant each day, you can't help but notice its fresh sprouts that have emerged overnight. Dropping a pinch of flakes into a fish tank, you welcome the creatures' graceful movements. With bird feeders placed outside windows, you familiarize yourself with the lives and communities of species and individual birds.

The growing research field of ecopsychology studies the effects of nature immersion on all areas of our health. An article from the

Yale School of Environment shares that it takes approximately two hours in nature for a person to feel healthy and a strong sense of well-being. The study explains that these two hours don't have to happen in one outing. When we spend a cumulative time of two hours within a week in outdoor spaces, there are significant health benefits. The summation is strong: doses of nature are restorative, healing, and life-giving. What if, along with our kids' daily vitamins, we give them a daily regimen of nature, both out-of-doors and inside? The research also shows that this two-hour mark is a rigid boundary. The study revealed that "there were no benefits for people who didn't meet that threshold."[4] Research is proving that exposure to nature decreases stress and anxiety, strengthens our immune systems, and builds confidence and self-esteem, to name only a few of the many benefits. Simply put, when we and our kids spend time with nature, we are calmer, focused, energized, creative, resilient, and happy. When we're surrounded by life, we feel more alive.

I can attest to the healing qualities of nature. Before we welcomed our daughter into our family, we lost a baby through miscarriage. In my grief, I turned to the outdoors. I needed God to meet me, so I went where I knew I could sense his presence: to the meadows, lakes, and woods. In hours spent along the trails, I found healing. The life cycles of the plants whispered a promise to my soul: new life comes after death. God is constantly making all things new. He brings beauty from hard soil. I experienced this healing power in the same way as God met me in my postpartum depression. With time spent outdoors and nature abounding indoors, I was surrounded by constant reminders of his tender care.

We saw this in the wake of the COVID-19 pandemic. When the world began shutting up its doors and people hunkered down inside, Colorado—and I'm sure many other places—did the opposite. We went outside. I have never seen our trails or natural areas busier. People wanted hope and healing, and they found it outside, much like young Anne Frank during the Nazi occupation. She wrote in her diary:

> The best remedy for those who are afraid, lonely or unhappy is to go outside, somewhere where they can be quiet, alone with the heavens, nature and God. Because only then does one feel that all is as it should be and that God wishes to see people happy, amidst the simple beauty of nature. As long as this exists, and it certainly always will, I know that then there will always be comfort for every sorrow, whatever the circumstances may be. And I firmly believe that nature brings solace in all troubles.[5]

The late president Theodore Roosevelt fled to the wilderness with a broken heart. On February 14, 1884, Roosevelt wrote in his journal, "The light has gone out of my life."[6] That morning his mother had passed away. Several hours later, in the very same house, his wife, who had recently fallen mysteriously ill, also died. The two women he loved most were gone in a matter of hours. It was a very dark Valentine's Day.

Roosevelt took the shattered remains of his spirit and walked into the wilderness, and that is where he began to heal. He went on to become a great conservationist establishing "150 national forests, 51 federal bird reserves, four national game preserves, five national parks and 18 national monuments on over 230 million acres of public land."[7]

He sought to protect the lands that he'd discovered hope in.

Something in our souls gravitates toward nature's restorative power. If our bodies are deficient in a particular nutrient, we crave certain foods. Similarly, our spirits crave nature when we need healing.

An obstacle to a nature-abundant life is access. Over the past decade, my family has inched closer and closer to the mountains. We have taken intentional steps and are now living in a place where we have constant access to natural areas, whether by car, bike, boat, or on foot. This was not always the case, however. We once lived on the third story of an old brick building in a dangerous neighborhood where it was unsafe to go for a walk around the block. Thankfully, it was a temporary situation. But it taught me to appreciate access to the outdoors. If you are living in a place that feels nature-deficient, take heart. There are ways to give your children nature-rich experiences wherever you are living. You can also be encouraged that society is beginning to recognize this deficiency and address it.

Realizing how incredible nature is for the health of individuals and communities, more and more people are promoting and working for access. Our local Nature in the City program is on a mission to provide open green spaces or natural settings within a ten-minute walking distance for every person in the community. I stood in one of their developed parks with a nature-inspired playground and path through a native plant pollinator garden. They repurposed what used to be a run-down and forgotten corner of our city and turned it into an inviting nature experience right in suburbia. Efforts like this are surfacing across the globe as we realize the necessity of natural areas and our ability to locate and get to them.

We can take this knowledge of nature's health benefits and create a sort of life hack in our homes. Although the most important thing is to step foot outdoors with our kids, we can complement that time by setting up our living areas as living spaces. We can guarantee the benefits of nature for our kids by providing them with access to nature all around our homes.

Coming from someone who has a borderline problem with collecting plants (I once adopted a potted tree with a Free sign on the side of the highway), I can attest to the power of nature in our living spaces. By bringing nature indoors, our kids not only get to see natural things on a daily basis, but they also have the opportunity to interact with it. They are immersed in close-contact creation. As they fill birdfeeders or water houseplants, they experience a direct connection to the God of the universe who tends to his creation. Here are some ways our family brings nature indoors.

### Tiny Terrariums

On a chilly winter day when we had been cooped up too long, my fingers ached to massage soil. The kids and I reached for supplies gathered earlier that week, and we set up a botanical "shop" at our dining room table. Before each child sat a glass jar. Spread amongst us was soil, sand, glass pebbles, dried moss, and small plants and succulents from a local greenhouse.

"We need a drainage layer first," I explained. "This layer soaks up liquid when we water our plants. You can use the sand or the glass pebbles."

My kids carefully selected their material and poured an initial layer into their jars.

"Good. Next, we can pour in some soil and select our plants," I explained.

Dirt-caked fingers reached across the table. They carefully scored roots and sowed transplants into the soil of their terrariums. We handled clumps of creeping thyme, succulents, asparagus fern, and strawberry begonias. Each plant presented a unique texture to our fingertips. When everyone had arranged their plants just right, we tucked moss between the gaps, forming a top layer to filter out toxins and keep the plants breathing cleanly.

Our home smelled like earth.

We talked about the importance of unique ecosystems and how different plants thrive in certain conditions.

"A terrarium of succulents and sand will need less watering. If you use tropical plants, they will need more water," I explained.

Our tiny terrariums reflected the ecosystem we're creating in our home. Just like the plants thriving in their ecosystems, God causes us to flourish where he has planted us. Sometimes, like the plants adorning our home, our leaves begin to wither. Stems turn brown. Flowers fail to blossom. But with careful tending, water, and sunlight, life rejuvenates. Roots strengthen. New sprouts press through. We now watch these processes from home as constant reminders of God bringing new life.

Download a free Terrarium Planting Activity and Bible Lesson on my website at www.erynlynum.com/terrarium.

❧

### Fresh-Cut Flowers

"Red represents respect, courage, and love." My friend Sally stood beside three massive buckets of freshly cut flowers and greenery.

"Dark pink shows gratitude and appreciation. Yellow means joy, happiness, and friendship. White represents innocence and loyalty. Green is for growth, nurturing, and harmony."

Four of us business-owning, Jesus-loving moms stood around the counter, eager to begin selecting flowers. At the onset of each new year, we spend three days together in the mountains to learn from one another, pray together, and dream for the coming year. At every retreat, we have a creative, hands-on activity Saturday evening, and this year, Sally, a professional floral designer, was teaching us how to arrange flowers. She came equipped with a bounty of blooms from her suppliers. We spent the evening carefully cleaning and arranging stems, experimenting with heights, shapes, and colors.

"This is so life-giving," I commented. We all agreed and planned occasional "flower therapy" gatherings together. We played with nature, feeling simultaneously like kids and artists. Have you ever interacted with flowers in such an intimate way? Such close contact with nature adjusts our souls and brings us nearer to our Creator.

The following week my daughter and I practiced what I had learned on the retreat. We stood in the grocery store's floral department and selected large magenta mum blossoms, along with delicate chamomile and fragrant eucalyptus. For fun and to "draw the eye through," as Sally would say, we added shiny bulbs of St. John's wort. At home, we grabbed vases and began carefully placing our greens in, followed by our flowers. This activity has become a regular connection point with my daughter. Each week after dropping her brothers at their homeschool program, she and I stop at the store and choose small bunches of flowers and greenery. Arriving home, we begin creating. Fresh-cut flowers adorn our home every week, and I see it affecting our family.

The boys were practicing drawing one day, creating detailed portrayals of home interiors. They sketched out still-life scenes with couches, wall hangings, and bookshelves. At the center of their tables, I spotted vases with fresh-cut flowers. That is when I realized the effect of a humble bunch of living things. The boys see it as an integral part of our home.

Download a Flower Arranging Family Guide + Bible Lesson on my website at www.erynlynum.com/flowers.

❧

### Raising Fish

When I was sixteen years old, a family friend was looking for summer help in his fish business, and I eagerly jumped at the opportunity. That summer, I learned about caring for both freshwater and saltwater tanks. I dipped my hands into the water with eels and poisonous lionfish. I cleaned the glass and added chemicals to the local library's freshwater tank. I visited nursing homes, private residences, and businesses to perform water changes on their tanks, admiring each unique watery world.

Those experiences and the passion for fishkeeping stayed with me. As soon as our sons were responsible enough, I shared it with them. We set up a tank for each boy and carefully selected species of aquatic critters. They learned how to choose fish that would get along well together, acclimate their fish to the water, monitor water temperatures, and observe their fish for signs of distress. Each boy practiced their water changes, siphoning old water into a bucket, then replenishing the tank with fresh water treated with the right chemicals.

Once our tanks were established and thriving, the boys were in for a treat.

"Mom! There is a baby fish!" my son exclaimed one morning.

I was sure he was mistaken. My fish knowledge lacked expertise in the area of live-bearing species, and I assumed all fish laid eggs. Yet when I walked over, the tiny wriggling creature was tucking itself in and out of the pebbles at the bottom of the tank.

"We need to go to the pet store!" I exclaimed. And off we went to purchase a "fish nursery." We placed the clear floating device into the tank then carefully scooped both mama and baby into it. A thin plastic wall separated them both, so mama wouldn't attempt to eat her baby for lunch. Raising wildlife affords our children many life lessons. All morning we watched as mama fish gave birth to tiny babies.

Not all of our fish endeavors have been so entertaining or lively. We have witnessed disease sweeping through our tanks, and we've scooped out our fair share of deceased fish. One son once lost his privilege to have a tank because of neglect. All of this provides valuable lessons to children. At the same time, it brings life to our home.

Rather than a television as the centerpiece of our living room, we have a fish tank with live plants and creatures. The warm glow of the light and the gracious movements of the fish add energy to an otherwise stagnant wall.

The hobby of fishkeeping is disappearing. We are hard-pressed to find tanks at businesses or in homes. Yet keeping fish is a fantastic opportunity to introduce our kids to the responsibility of nurturing life and the wonder of having nature in our homes. It is easy to be overwhelmed with where to start or what species to select. Prior experiences of upside-down floating fish deter us. Yet a short conversation with an aquatic specialist at a fish store goes a long way in being successful fish hobbyists. Watching my kids ask the fish store staff questions was an amazing experience. Where my kids gravitated toward the shape or color of certain species, the staff kindly guided them toward other options for hardiness and ease of care. Fishkeeping affords us yet another opportunity to discover how nature thrives in the right conditions, just as God created us to flourish under his tender care. Here are some tips for beginning fish raisers:

1. Begin medium: A too-large tank can be overwhelming, and a too-small tank has a fragile ecosystem that is more difficult to balance. A twenty- to thirty-gallon tank is a great starter size.
2. Begin fresh: Saltwater tanks can be costly and have a delicate ecosystem. Become comfortable in freshwater tanks before attempting a saltwater tank.
3. Begin simple: The basic things you will need are a tank with a lid and built-in light, a submersible fish tank heater, a filter, pebbles, some decorations, a water conditioner to make tap water healthy for fish, and fish themselves! You can find a complete starter kit with most if not everything but the fish.
4. Begin with help: The greatest thing we've ever done in fishkeeping is talking with experts. If possible, locate an aquatics store

wholly dedicated to fish rather than a broader large-scale pet store. A pet store will do, and their aquatics specialist will be helpful. But we have found that an actual fish-dedicated store has more expertise and varieties of fish. Be completely honest that you're just starting. They want to help, and they want to introduce kids to this lively hobby! Ask for recommendations on how many fish to have in your size tank and what varieties to pair together.

5. Begin with easy species: I have heartier species like tetras and barbs in my tank. Kids often gravitate toward fun shapes, energetic movements, and vivid colors. For my kids, I love species like platys and live-bearing mollies. Ask an aquatics specialist what varieties to avoid. Some fish only do well with their own species or in a particular tank size.

6. Begin slowly: Acclimate your tank by setting it up, establishing bacteria (an aquatics specialist can guide you to the product and information for this), and starting with a few "tester fish" like neon tetras. Once the water balance is correct (which an aquatic specialist can easily test for you at the store when you bring in a sample), begin introducing more fish. The first three weeks as you establish your tank offer a great lesson in patience for your kids.

❧

### Bringing Birds In

Let me preface this activity with this caveat: the birds are, of course, outdoors. But you can bring them in as close as you can! Watching my kids watch birds, I've witnessed a deep connection to God and his whimsical designs. My kids come alive when they observe the lives of birds. In his book *The Home Place*, author J. Drew Lanham writes,

"I felt closer to flight by bringing the birds nearer to my earthbound existence."[8]

A few years ago, we lived in a new home in a newly developed subdivision. Each new house had one tree in the front yard, with branches barely able to support a bird's nest. A line of mature cottonwood trees stood at the edge of our development, however. We knew birds were there; we just had to convince them to come close. My husband hung bird feeders before we even had a fence or yard set up. Slowly, red-winged blackbirds, sparrows, and grackles arrived. Each morning we would discover more birds at the feeders. We even glimpsed hummingbirds and migrating Bullock's orioles throughout the first summer. My favorite bird visit was from a Cooper's hawk. These hawks are part of a larger collection of birds known as accipiters, or small "backyard" raptors. My husband spotted him balanced on our back fence and called me over quickly to see. With his arrival, I knew we had succeeded in bringing the birds in.

A couple of years later, when we moved to our current home, I was overwhelmed with the birding opportunities. Living by a lake, we watch water birds. Having fields adjacent to our neighborhood, we have field and prairie birds. With trees all around, we welcome songbirds, owls, and many other species. Again, before we had much of our home or yard set up, my husband hung feeders all around. My favorite two feeders are outside my office window, where I watch chickadees feed throughout the day as I work and write. My other favorite feeder is directly outside our kitchen window. Working in the kitchen, I have sparrows, jays, juncos, and towhees snacking three feet from my face. If anything can make a task like dishwashing enjoyable, it's doing it with the birds.

Our kids often sit at the dining room table watching our avian neighbors arrive for breakfast at the feeders outside our windows. We are all becoming more familiar with each species and its antics.

My eleven-year-old son loves watching out my office window and glimpsing the starling that lives in a hole in our white poplar.

Whether you live in an area rich with trees and bird habitat, or in a development with few trees to speak of, hang feeders and see what visits. Begin with various feeders and foods to see which birds prefer what for lunch. Visit a local bird store or farm store and gather advice on how to bring in local species. As the birds come, hang a chalkboard on the wall alongside binoculars and a local bird species guide, and begin identifying and writing down which species you see.

## Bringing Nature Indoors

By bringing nature inside, we can capture the awe of creation more closely, within the confines of our own homes. You can create a beautiful atmosphere and ecosystem that will affect your children for the rest of their lives.

I have struggled over time with how much nature to bring inside. At one point, my husband had to finally limit our fish tanks (one apiece for the kids and me), although he never dares put a limit on my houseplants. We nearly began a chicken-raising operation before realizing it wasn't the season for us to do so. Although I want to raise goats, I know that too must wait. There is a time and place for these endeavors. But I think if we're always afraid of adding "just one more thing to keep alive," we miss out on creative and life-giving opportunities to bless our homes with nature.

There is a balance to strike here. I involve my kids as much as I can in the upkeep of our indoor ecosystems. I also choose easier things to care for. Our fish require food every day and a water change every few weeks. My plants need watering one to two times a week. Although it can feel at times like more chores, for the most part, tending to living things gives life to our spirits.

I recently spent a morning repotting our plants. A couple of them had died, and others were thriving and outgrowing their pots. Bringing each of them outside, I spent a couple of hours fitting them into larger pots, arranging soil, and then watering. My daughter, at four years old, was eager to help. She grabbed a tiny container and made her way to the hose. Little by little, she kept arriving and watering each plant.

Nurturing life with our kids is therapeutic and life-giving. By digging fingers into dirt next to theirs, or silently observing a tree sparrow's morning routine, we get to interact with creation alongside our children. We can create meaningful moments right at home while learning about our Maker and engaging with his wonders.

## *Step Outside*

Using nature to decorate your home is a quick and effective way to expose your children to God's creation on a daily basis. Potted plants, a fish tank, and a birdfeeder outside the window offer immediate benefits for the health of your children, home, and family. Begin creating an ecosystem of living things right where your family eats, sleeps, and does life. This is especially advantageous during winter months (or summer if you live in an extremely hot climate), when we tend to be indoors more. Start incorporating nature into your home and including your children in the care of these things. Watch how it affects the disposition of your family and the culture of your home.

### See Nature in the Bible

Was there a difficult time in your life that you can look back on and see that you—whether intentionally or not—sought healing and hope in nature? It is powerful to show our children how God created nature to help our minds, bodies, and spirits be healthy. Explore with them the following Scriptures where God used nature to bless and heal:

- Jeremiah 31:2 says that after Israel survived the sword, they "found grace in the wilderness."

- Psalm 72:3 (NASB) reads, "May the mountains bring peace to the people."
- Luke 5:16 says, "Jesus Himself would *often* slip away to the wilderness and pray" (NASB, emphasis added). Ask your children why they think Jesus chose to pray outside in nature.
- Isaiah 55:12 says, "For you shall go out in joy and be led forth in peace; the mountains and the hills before you shall break forth into singing, and all the trees of the field shall clap their hands."

### See God in Nature

If you prefer to begin bringing nature indoors with something demanding less attention (read: doesn't need to be fed), take part in the old German tradition known as *Wunderkammer*, as described in chapter 8, in which self-proclaimed museum curators collected fun and fascinating discoveries from nature and displayed them across shelves, tables, and entire corners of their houses.

Kids are naturally adept at this *Wunderkammer* type of collecting. Spare yourself frustrations of finding old animal bones, rocks, and wilted leaves under couches and in closets. Instead, encourage and equip your kids to collect nature by providing display stations.

Thrift stores are one of our favorite places to find unique displays. We once found an old poker table—a perfect square coffee table with a large pull-out drawer, lined with green velvet, with a glass top—where our children house their fossils, similar to a glass display in a museum. We also found a wooden swivel display with twelve open-top drawers for rocks. Go thrifting, get creative, and set up displays for rocks, fossils, feathers, shells, and other finds from outside. Let your children create a Cabinet of Wonders where they can collect, display, and study the details of God's magnificent creations up close!

— 13 —

# Unshakable Faith

*Reading about nature is fine, but if a person walks in the woods and listens carefully, he can learn more than what is in books, for they speak with the voice of God.*

GEORGE WASHINGTON CARVER

THERE IS A DIFFICULT TENSION we face when helping our children in their faith journey. Yet this tension is an opportunity to equip our kids with resilient faith. Our kids—just like us—have to grapple with the fact that certain facets of faith cannot be seen.

As we help our children familiarize themselves with what we *can* see—the convincing evidence in nature for our Creator—we help them bridge a gap between doubt and a faith with substance. They come to peace with the intangible pieces of faith as they discover the repertoire of hints, clues, and facts God left us throughout history and in science. Walking with them over that bridge of evidence, we discover an unshakable faith founded on facts, rooted in God's Word, and strengthened by experiences with God in creation.

I witnessed this strengthening of faith in September 2021.

Across the country, my grandma lay dying in her apartment. My mother stood at her bedside, walking with her mother through her final days. At the realization that Gram was not "coming back around" this time, I knew I, too, needed to go be with her.

But for four years, intense anxiety about flying had tethered me to the ground. Undiagnosed vertigo gave way to feelings of panic when flying. "I don't fly" became my self-limiting mantra.

But now, Gram was dying, and God was telling me to go see her.

I told my husband I would take our oldest son.

"As a therapy child?" Grayson asked.

*Yes.* Someone to distract me from the gripping anxiety.

We woke at 4:30 a.m. to a waxing crescent moon. As we drove an hour south to the airport, the moon, hardly a sliver, groggily peeked out from a shadowed sphere. Gradually, as we drove, it was swallowed by the light of the rising sun. The eastern horizon glowed pink, nudging the mountains to the west awake.

Grayson hugged me on the curb.

I leaned into the back seat of the SUV. "I'll see you in two days," I told our three youngest.

My oldest slung his backpack over his shoulder and headed into the airport. He hadn't flown in seven years. Yet he looked braver than me as we made our way through security and to our gate.

He sat beside me as the plane accelerated down the runway. He held my hand.

Once in the air, I pointed out the window. "Look at that."

He already was.

We stared at puffy cloud towers. They stretched vertically, waxing and waning like a lava lamp. It's on these rare occasions that we are afforded the vantage point of a bird. Before the invention of planes, without this perspective, would anyone believe the clouds rise in such a way as this? We have trouble believing what we can't see with our own eyes.

My mom picked us up at the airport and took us the rest of the way to the apartment. We hadn't told Gram we were coming. Standing at her bedside, I wondered if she was lucid.

Her foggy eyes looked up and caught mine. She stared—confused—but sure. "Eryn!" She pulled me into her feeble arms and wept.

I wept too. Surety filled my soul. I was where I needed to be.

Over the following two days, I watched my mom and aunt do one of the bravest things I've ever witnessed: care for my grandma. Every moment I could, I sat at Gram's side, holding her hand, smoothing back her still-black hair. When I needed to use the restroom or make a meal, my oldest son sat vigil. Watching someone die is not easy; not at thirty-one years old, and certainly not at ten. Pride filled my heart as I watched him hold Gram's hand and chat with her.

Gram was scared. Only a week before she had chosen to accept Jesus as her Savior. Her faith was young, and although she had peace that she was about to enter heaven, she had trouble envisioning what was coming. Her faith was new, and it faltered in the face of uncertainty. She knew she would be with my grandpa soon. She would meet Jesus. But how would it all unfold? What happens between this deathbed and that glory? She could not picture it, which made her very afraid.

"I had a baby," she told me.

I knew. I'd heard snippets of this story. Now she told me more as we watched hummingbirds collecting pollen from flowers outside her window. She's always loved hummingbirds.

"His name was Johnny. He only lived thirteen days." She was crying now. I was too.

How many times over the decades had she shed tears for this child? *They are nearly out, Gram, these tears for Johnny. You're almost done crying for him.*

"I'm going to go see him soon," she told me. Or perhaps she was reassuring herself.

"Soon," I agreed.

A couple of days later, when I would return home, my children would ask me, "What is it like when we die and go to heaven?" They would ask about the process, that final journey.

"It's like we close our eyes, then when we open them, we'll see Jesus," I would tell them.

But right now, still at Gram's side, watching her sleep, I questioned what heaven is like. Have you ever tried to imagine what comes after this life, and found the gaps and unknowns filling with uncertainty and doubt? Gram was about to experience something for which none of us has context. No one can tell an "I remember when . . ." story of going to heaven. It can be difficult to believe when we have no recollection or experience of something.

When Gram napped, my mom, my son, and I took walks outside, picking flowers and sorting our thoughts about life, death, and faith. I prayed for one more conversation with Gram. When she awoke after napping all afternoon, Gram and I sat for two hours, recollecting.

"I have to leave tomorrow," I told her, tears welling in my eyes.

"I know," she told me. "You need to get back to Grayson and the kids." She held my hand; she understood. I kissed her forehead, and, her eyes still closed, she lifted a smile.

Come morning, the plane lifted with the sunrise over Pittsburgh. The sun was beginning its daily ascent. Morning condensation gathered and hovered along the river, waiting to ascend, right along with the sun, higher into the sky. My son and I stared out the window.

Like the cloud towers two days before, I felt this is something we're not supposed to see from above; morning's mist winding over the water like a blanket. Yet even before the Wright Brothers' ingenuity gave birth to a winged machine, the cloud towers built in the sky each day. Fog hugged the river's surface each morning.

Just because we didn't have this perspective from above doesn't mean it wasn't happening. William Paley once wrote, "The uncertainty of one thing does not necessarily affect the certainty of another thing. Our ignorance of many points need not suspend our assurance of a few."[1] Just because we've never touched heaven doesn't mean it's not waiting for us.

We flew back to Denver. My mom and aunt held my gram's hands; they got her where she needed to be. A week later, she was with Grandpa, Jesus, and baby Johnny.

I have watched people struggle with their faith. I have grappled with my own. Yet I had never sat at the bedside of someone as they were dying. I had never heard their unguarded doubts as they stood at the edge of eternity. There were moments when Gram was so terrified of what was coming, a shadow she could not escape. Yet in other moments, she was entirely sure and ready. If I'm honest, I sometimes feel the same, a juxtaposition of doubt and confidence.

Have you felt this wavering in your own faith or sensed doubts in your children as they grapple with what to believe in an ever-changing world? Some aspects of faith are intangible. We cannot see them. Yet we read in John 20:29, "Blessed are those who have not seen and yet have believed." Going back to Hebrews 11:1, we're reminded that despite what's unseen, we have evidence for God. The verse tells us, "Now faith is the assurance of things hoped for, the conviction of things not seen." Remember that the root word for *assurance* means "substance," and the word for *conviction* refers to "evidence." It is true that we cannot prove every aspect of our faith in a test tube or glass beaker. But we can equip our children with a resilient and unshakable faith by providing them every evidence we have available. Like my son glimpsing cloud towers and fog banks from above, our kids, as they experience nature from new angles and perspectives, will gather a collection of evidence for who God is and how he loves them, much like Abram found new perspective when God met him in Hebron.

## "He Brought Him Outside"

Travel back to that starry night, when God made his covenant promise to Abram. In their interaction we can see how fundamental an outdoor experience was to Abram's faith. The same is true for our children. Every adventure outside provides them opportunity to engage with God and develop their faith.

In Genesis 15:5 we read that God "brought him outside."

We can learn a lot from God's example here. Powerful things happen when we take our children outside. We step away from a human-made domain and into God's wild world that reflects his glory.

God took Abram out into the open air, and he offers the same invitation today to you and your children. God knew Abram needed to see the stars to believe. He needed a visual to anchor his faith in.

Verses five and six tell us: "And he brought him outside and said, 'Look toward heaven, and number the stars, if you are able to number them.' Then he said to him, 'So shall your offspring be.' And he believed the LORD, and he counted it to him as righteousness."

The night sky was the catalyst for Abram's faith. What might be the catalyst for your children's faith? What will their "Hebron experience" be? Maybe it will be a walk along the river, a hike through the woods, or a night sleeping beneath the stars. Perhaps it will be many of these things strung together over the course of their childhood. The more of these experiences you give your children, the more opportunity they will have to know God's nearness, beauty, and power.

As Abram discovered, the night sky can be quite convincing. The day sky can be also—especially when it looks like night. This is what I witnessed during my own Hebron experience.

On August 21, 2017, we stood atop a sand dune in Newport, Oregon. We were entirely out of our element. Over the past three days, Grayson and I and our three boys had caravanned west. Less than a week before, we'd sold our home, purchased a well-used twenty-foot travel trailer, and set out on a nine-week adventure to the Pacific

Northwest. We set our first map marker on Newport, Oregon, where we would arrive in perfect time to witness the solar eclipse from within the "Totality Zone."

I had little idea of what this eclipse totality meant.

Along our drive, as forest fires hemmed around our route, we considered shifting trajectory and heading north to Washington. Surely, we could see the phenomena from a few hundred miles up the map, out of totality, and it would still be neat. We watched fire maps on the screens of our phones, making best guesses as to which directions the flames would travel and how heavy the smoke might become. We decided to keep on route, and eventually, smoke gave way to wet salty air. We camped in a grossly overpriced parking lot with no electrical or plumbing hookups.

The eclipse had driven up prices anywhere near these totality hot spots. Cardboard signs with permanent markers dotted each town: "Eclipse parking, $20!" and "Special event T-Shirts," and in front of one restaurant, "Join us for the end of the world!" At $98 a night, this boat-storage-lot-turned-eclipse-campground would be the most expensive place we parked our camper over our entire trip. But on the morning of the eclipse, that expense turned into an investment of a lifetime.

"Mom, can we decorate these?" Our oldest sat at our small, foldable dining room table next to his brothers on the upholstered benches.

Each child held a paper plate with small eye holes cut out of the middle. These paper plates would be taped to the special "Eclipse Event Sunglasses" my parents mailed us a few weeks prior when we still had a home address. The thick paper surrounding the eyeglasses would serve as extra protection as they stared directly into the sun.

As the boys decorated their masks, morning fog began to drift out to sea, revealing a clear sky. And then, just before ten in the morning as the eclipse began, the fog reversed direction, rushing back in around us. It felt supernatural yet was completely natural in an extraordinary way.

We grabbed our eclipse glasses, snapped the leash on our Labrador, and climbed the sand dune behind our trailer. Fellow sojourners waited with us, setting up camp chairs to our left and right. I wondered if they, too, had traveled for days. I noticed we were the only ones with small children in tow. I thought of several friends back home in Colorado who'd pulled their kids out of school for the day and driven through the night just to hit a spot near totality.

We waited as an eerie silence overtook the bay.

The warm August air was plummeting to evening temperature as the sun began to disappear. Seagulls began screeching. Sea lions down on the docks joined in the clamor with the birds. Nature gained volume, but every human fell silent as the earth darkened. Blacker and blacker the world fell. Planes in the sky left course and turned sharp to give passengers a view of the anomaly. It felt like an apocalypse film, but we stood our sandy ground. Jet trails zigzagged, turning pink like clouds in a setting sun, then disappeared into the false night. And then the sun itself disappeared, leaving stars gleaming in the blackened midmorning sky. Remnants of sunlight fought to break around the centerpiece moon. On our hill and across the bay, onlookers began to shout and cheer, but my breath held.

"How does God do that?" our four-year-old asked.

The moon eclipsed the sun, and as it aligned, something within me began to align also. For one minute and forty-five seconds on that hilltop, God grasped my heart and showed me anew his power and majesty. A God whose glory will not be hidden. A God who hung those stars, that sun, and the moon in the sky. And while he did, he was thinking of me, of my husband and three boys, and of the new life that was beating in my womb.

"Look toward heaven," God had told Abram.

I heard it too on that sandy hilltop. Abram and I both looked heavenward.

"And he believed the Lord."

It appears God is still using the night sky to woo us.

It wasn't only the wonder of the eclipse we witnessed that day. What we saw was direct evidence for a Creator. When we have these emotional and awestruck moments in nature, we can dig further to learn about the designs that make them possible and use those experiences to point our children to God. When I began learning about solar eclipses, it became more than just a personal experience. The facts rooted my faith deeper.

Solar eclipses throughout history have guided scientific investigation and discoveries, including Einstein's theory of general relativity, the rate at which the earth's rotation is slowing down and how our planet's surface is changing, as well as deciphering ancient calendars and developing historical timelines in human history.[2] In *Science and the Mind of the Maker*, Melissa Cain Travis explains the rare phenomenon of our total eclipses. For a total eclipse to happen, where the moon passes between the earth and the sun and completely blocks out our view of the sun, the earth, sun, and moon have to be the perfect size, shape, and distance from one another. It just so happens ours are. Not only that, but they are positioned to put on the magnificent display my husband and kids and I witnessed that day, with an eclipse long enough for us to observe and study.

Travis explains that total eclipses are temporary because the moon used to be closer to Earth and is gradually distancing itself from our planet. It is a show with numbered seasons. Yet humanity exists within a perfect timeframe for us to observe these total eclipses. When we consider that eclipses have aided in significant scientific discoveries and understanding about how our planet and the universe work, it's incredible to think that God placed all of this into perfect timing for us to witness, study, and learn more about who he is. Cain summarizes with these words: "Isn't it a curious thing that mankind is thriving during the window of time that perfect eclipses are an available (and invaluable) tool for scientific discovery?" She goes on to share a quote from the book *The Privileged Planet*, which says, "The most habitable place in the Solar System yields the best view of solar eclipses just when observers can best appreciate them."[3]

Standing beneath a black morning sky, the moon, for a moment, stealing the show, I had to agree. It's a curious thing.

In her book *Vesper Flights*, author Helen Macdonald writes about these total solar eclipses. She does not approach the topic from the standpoint of God as Creator. Yet in her words, we sense a change in inflection; awe regarding the divine nature of a total eclipse. She shares her experience watching the sun disappear behind a black disc, then reemerging: "For it turns out there's something even more affecting than watching the sun disappear into a hole . . . from the lower edge of the blank, black disc of the dead sun, bursts a perfect point of brilliance. It leaps and burns. It's unthinkably fierce, unbearably bright, something (I blush to say it, but here it comes) like a word. And thus begins the world again."[4]

Something *like a word*.

It brings to mind John 1:1 where Jesus is called "the Word": "In the beginning was the Word, and the Word was with God, and the Word was God." A few chapters later in John 8:12, we see Jesus as the light: "Again Jesus spoke to them, saying, 'I am the light of the world. Whoever follows me will not walk in darkness, but will have the light of life.'" I imagine as Helen Macdonald stood beneath the solar eclipse, watching a "perfect point of brilliance" bursting forth from behind the moon, she experienced something similar to what I did as I watched the eclipse with my family. Light always wins, as we see in John 1:5: "The light shines in the darkness, and the darkness has not overcome it."

Imagine years after God made a promise to Abram beneath innumerable stars. When he was wealthy and blessed, what thoughts might have run through his mind every time he stood beneath a night sky. God rooted his promise to Abram in a tangible visual as a nightly reminder. Consider how in every trial he faced, in each doubt and uncertainty, the night sky revived his faith. I imagine him, on a difficult night, looking over to his son Isaac, promise in flesh form, then lifting his gaze to the heavens.

These visuals anchor truths in our minds, hearts, and souls. Our beliefs are often pressed, stretched, and weathered by fear and unknowns. The Bible is clear that we will face many hazards to our faith. If we don't equip our kids with solid evidence for their beliefs, doubts may swallow them. On the other hand, as they discover all the proof we have for a creator God, then when questions arise, deception lurks, and trials chip away at their belief system, it won't crumble. The tangible attributes of nature give our children something to hold on to, something mirroring a partial reflection of the intangible attributes of God.

Our kids can have a faith like that of 1 Peter 1:6–7: "For a little while, if necessary, you have been grieved by various trials, so that the tested genuineness of your faith—more precious than gold that perishes though it is tested by fire—may be found to result in praise and glory and honor at the revelation of Jesus Christ."

The Greek word here, *dokimion*, translated as *genuineness*, means "tested proof" and "trustworthiness." When the infernos of life's challenges rage, may the impurities of doubt and false ideas be burned away, and our children's faith remain unscathed, intact, and genuine.

## May Our Kids See, Know, and Consider

You are qualified to teach your children who God is through what he has made. Your own childhood outdoor experiences don't qualify you. Your knowledge of natural things doesn't qualify you. Your familiarity with the Bible doesn't qualify you. All of these things can help, but ultimately it is God who qualifies you, as we read in 2 Corinthians 3:5, "Not that we are sufficient in ourselves to claim anything as coming from us, but our sufficiency is from God." As you draw near to God and ask him to teach you about himself, he will equip you to help your children see, know, and consider who he is.

In *A Sand County Almanac*, Aldo Leopold shares the story of a young child who came to a belief in God after observing warblers. After watching my sons caught up in wonder with these magnificent, colorful migratory birds, I resonate with the story. Leopold wrote:

> I heard of a boy once who was brought up an atheist. He changed his mind when he saw that there were a hundred-odd species of warblers, each bedecked like to the rainbow, and each performing yearly sundry thousands of miles of migration about which scientists wrote wisely but did not understand. No "fortuitous concourse of elements" working blindly through any number of millions of years could quite account for why warblers are so beautiful. No mechanistic theory, even bolstered by mutations, has ever quite answered for the colors of the cerulean warbler, or the vespers of the woodthrush, or the swansong. . . . I dare say this boy's convictions would be harder to shake than those of many inductive theologians. There are yet many boys to be born who, like Isaiah, "may see and know and consider, and understand together, that the hand of the Lord hath done this."

Birds—and every other thing God has bedecked in the natural world—hold power to convince our kids of his presence and activity in the world. Leopold then asked this poignant question: "But where shall they see, and know, and consider? In museums?"[5]

Let me pause for a moment on the topic of museums. Have you

ever watched your children's imaginations come alive while exploring a museum? In these places they have unique opportunities to see up close and interact with so many rare and even extinct pieces of God's creation. I watched this happen with my own kids when we visited a dinosaur museum on my oldest son's eighth birthday.

"You guys, come here, touch this." I invited the boys over to an interactive exhibit. An original—not a casted mimic—dinosaur bone sat kid-level on display. "You're touching something that is years upon years upon years old."

My sons' eyes grew wider with each repetition of my words.

"Can you imagine," I asked them, "if paleontologists hadn't worked so hard to find and preserve all of these fossils? We would never know God made them."

Their little hands remained steady on the fossil.

I continued, "If we're not careful to protect our parks and natural areas, years from now, people might not know about all that we have right now."

Museums offer unique opportunities to teach our children about things God has made that have since been lost in time. These lessons percolate in our children's minds, creating a sense of wonder and an urgency to protect what we still have.

But Leopold's question still stands, begging an answer. Are museums the only places our children will experience a connection to their Creator? Leopold highlights the important words of Isaiah 41:20: "That they may see and know, may consider and understand together, that the hand of the LORD has done this." You might be asking, isn't there more to see, know, consider, and understand?

## Nature Matures Our Faith

We cannot depend only on what others have written in books or preserved in museum displays to teach our kids about God's wonders. These resources are helpful, but they lack an intimate element of engagement. Your children's faith will strengthen as they spend time directly encountering God's wild world.

Our kids are encountering age-old false ideas repackaged in modern deceptions. They are growing up in a world of confused values or no values at all. In Ephesians 4:14–15, we find a powerful prayer for this generation: "That we may no longer be children, tossed to and fro by the waves and carried about by every wind of doctrine, by human cunning, by craftiness in deceitful schemes. Rather, speaking the truth in love, we are to grow up in every way into him who is the head, into Christ."

Tying biblical truth to historical and scientific evidence helps our children to "grow up in every way" into Christ. In 1 Corinthians 3:2, the apostle Paul is speaking to immature believers. He tells them, "I fed you with milk, not solid food, for you were not ready for it." Milk is necessary for a time. If you have raised an infant, you know how true this is. But they don't stay on milk. In time, with careful training, they move on to solid food. It is the same with our faith . . . or is it? That is up to us. Let us not release our kids into the world with bellies full of milk. Experiences in nature mature our children's faith as they discover evidences for their Creator.

Early in September, we drove an old fire road far back into the mountains. We stopped at a small grove of trees with a creek running through it. We strung up a hammock, set up our camp chairs, unzipped a cooler of snacks, and grabbed our books. For the entire afternoon, we read, played, and meandered through the trees.

Contrasting beauty lives in many of these places we explore. Black wildfire scars punctuate our area of the map. To one side of us was a hillside of dead trees, life sapped by the invasive pine beetle. These trees are matchsticks waiting to light up. On the other side was a graveyard of already burned trees, devoured by fire years ago. And beneath them, new pine and aspen saplings stretched toward the sky, carpeting the deadened forest floor with a promise of new life.

"It's crazy," my oldest wondered aloud, "how much death and how much life can be together."

Only the forest places thoughts like these in a child's mind.

That afternoon, driving between rows of pine, my son remarked that "they look like kings."

"Like they have crowns," his little brother added. The trees arced over, top-heavy with boughs of pine and cones at their tips.

"And they're bowing down," my oldest concluded.

In nature, we join in their worship. Psalm 96:12 paints a similar picture: "Let the field exult, and everything in it! Then shall all the trees of the forest sing for joy."

In God's creation is where our children "see and know . . . consider and understand together, that the hand of the LORD has done this." God invites us into this natural classroom offering a robust education about who he is. Out here we get to infuse an unshakable faith in our children as they explore creation at their own pace and led by their curiosity.

The more we familiarize ourselves with nature, considering its ways, details, and offerings, the deeper we know our Maker. As our kids become comfortable with copious amounts of time outside, they will experience God in a way no indoor lessons can offer. Their faith will gain depth and resilience. No matter life's demands and challenges, they'll have a reserve of experiences to draw from in the years to come.

Let us return to the meadow where this story began. Imagine yourself with me and my family in that very meadow right now. The elk are again bugling across sweeping valleys. It is a different year, and our third time coming up to witness the elk rut. The sun is lingering around the campsite, giving one final stretch across the sky before it slips behind Long's Peak, the tallest mountain around. Soup is on. I hear our boys laughing in the woods.

Our daughter sits next to the campfire, nibbling cornbread. A curious chipmunk peeks out from the rock beside her, eyeing her snack.

After dinner, we meander along the river before the meadow is closed for the evening to allow the elk a safe passage. Tall grass brushes our legs. The kids toss stones into the water.

We lose all sense of time.

A bull elk's eerie call travels through the valley. The native grasses trade it off, blade by blade, until it reaches another bull, which immediately responds. We watch the sun swap places with the moon.

These mountain experiences are not normal, everyday scenarios. They're the cream on top, and they're worth every effort to make happen. But the truth is, resilient faith takes shape in the day-to-day experiences. It is in a succession of ordinary nature exposures that your children's faith will grow and flourish. If one day they stand before a sprawling ocean, beneath an expanse of stars, or surrounded by mountain summits, it will serve as a confirmation of what they've discovered through more ordinary experiences of climbing a tree, playing in a creek, or splashing in rain puddles. Right now, you have what you need to equip your children with a resilient faith rooted in the wonder of creation. It begins by opening God's Word and stepping out into his world. As you anchor your children's memories into nature's soil, you will help them reconnect the dots between creation and Creator.

Beneath the rocks, in hollowed logs, and carried by a sparrow's song, may your children discover an unshakable faith.

## Step Outside

Here we are at the final Step Outside section, only I hope this is not an ending, but a beginning. May this be where you and your children discover a robust and resilient faith anchored in outdoor adventures. I want to challenge you to *step outside* and create space and opportunity for your children's "Hebron experience." Rather than trying to orchestrate something big, simply give them every opportunity to meet with their Creator that they may see, know, and consider all he has made, and what it means for our faith and lives. May they, like Abram, stare into creation and believe. Here is my prayer for today's kids, including yours and mine:

> Creator God, our heavenly Father,
>
> As you long to meet our kids, we ache for them to know and follow you. Call them outside to explore your world and reconnect the dots between creation and Creator. Fill them with wonder that compels them to explore your world. Fuel their God-given curiosity and make it contagious to those around them. Lead them to the hints you've left throughout creation that will pique their interests.
>
> As they fall in love with what you have made, infuse them with purpose in protecting and preserving your art. Show them in the contours and contrasts of creation that you are not a wishy-washy God but a loving Father who has life-giving boundaries and great plans for our lives. Call them into creation to sort their minds and think upon everything lovely and true. Anchor their memories in the scents, colors, textures, flavors, and songs of nature. Show them time as a gift and create urgency in their souls to spend it well, allotting vast chunks of their days to exploring all you have made.
>
> In nature, may they accept your invitation to a restful and peaceful life, aligning their pace to nature's rhythms. Awaken the creative spirit you've placed inside them and use your designs and art to inspire their endeavors. When they face difficulties and hardships, may they discover refuge and healing in your Word and in nature. In every unknown and doubt, point them to what we know is true and all the evidence we have for your existence and love. Lord, in all of this, meet our kids outside and nurture our family's faith through your creation. Amen.

# Resources

**Group Study Guide: Nurture Your Family's Faith with Friends!**
Download the Group Study Guide and invite your book club, parenting group, church group, homeschool group, hiking buddies, or friends to journey through *Rooted in Wonder* together!

www.ErynLynum.com/RootedinWonder

❧

**Free Downloadable Resources & Activities**
Begin stepping outside and spending intentional time with your children as you build an unshakable faith! Find inspiration in these free downloads from my website.

www.ErynLynum.com/free

**God of Wonders Devotional**
*Five Lessons from Nature for Teaching Your Child Who God Is and How He Loves Them*

## Terrarium Planting Nature + Bible Activity
*With Accompanying Devotional: Learning to Thrive Where God Plants Us*

## A Guide to Identify and Live by Your Family Values
*A Step-by-Step Guide for Parents and Caregivers*

## Flower Arranging Family Guide + Bible Lesson
*Teach Your Child How God Makes Us Unique While Arranging Flowers by Their Meaning*

❧

## Recommended Books for You and Your Child
Add substance to your child's faith through evidences found in history and science and told through the stories of those who have gone before us. Find our recommended reading list on my website.

### www.ErynLynum.com/bookshelf

# Notes

### Fully Convinced

1. As quoted in John Hudson Tiner, *Johannes Kepler: Giant of Faith and Science*, The Sowers (Fenton: Mott Media, 1993), 73.

### Chapter 1: This Is My Father's World

1. Kenneth W. Osbeck, *101 Hymn Stories: The Inspiring True Stories Behind 101 Favorite Hymns* (Grand Rapids: Kregel Publications, 2012), 98.
2. Conor Knighton, *Leave Only Footprints: My Acadia-to-Zion Journey Through Every National Park* (New York: Crown, 2020), 62.
3. C. S. Lewis, *The Four Loves* (New York: Harcourt, Brace & World, 1960), 20.
4. Melissa Cain Travis, *Science and the Mind of the Maker: What the Conversation between Faith and Science Reveals about God* (Eugene, OR: Harvest House Publishers, 2018), 34.
5. Travis, *Science and the Mind of the Maker*, 82.
6. Matthew Sleeth, *Reforesting Faith: What Trees Teach Us about the Nature of God and His Love for Us* (Colorado Springs: WaterBrook, 2019), 99.

**Chapter 2: Reconnecting the Dots Between Creation and Creator**

1. Aldo Leopold, *A Sand County Almanac* (New York: Ballantine Books, 1966), 28.

2. Charlotte Mason, *The Outdoor Life of Children: The Importance of Nature Study and Outside Activities*, Charlotte Mason Topics (Independently published, 2015, from Charlotte Mason's works in the public domain), 10.

3. Web.archive.org, Paduae, August 19, 1610. Archived July 18, 2011, at the Wayback Machine (in Latin). Original Latin text: Antonio Favaro, *Le Opere di Galileo Galilei.*

4. David L. Block and Kenneth C. Freeman, *God and Galileo: What a 400-Year-Old Letter Teaches Us about Faith and Science* (Wheaton: Crossway, 2019), 32.

5. As quoted in John Hudson Tiner, *Johannes Kepler: Giant of Faith and Science*, The Sowers (Fenton: Mott Media, 1993), 152.

6. Block & Freeman, *God and Galileo*, 32.

7. Paul David Tripp, *Awe: Why It Matters for Everything We Think, Say, and Do* (Wheaton: Crossway, 2015), 66.

8. Stephen O'Doherty, "The Case For Christ: Journalist Lee Strobel's Personal Journey," interview with Lee Strobel, published April 12, 2017, https://hope1032.com.au/stories/faith/2017/case-christ-journalist-lee-strobel-personal-journey/.

9. David C. Downing, *The Most Reluctant Convert: C. S. Lewis's Journey to Faith*, C. S. Lewis Secondary Studies Series (Eugene, OR: Wipf and Stock, 2021), 11.

10. Robert B. Stewart, "C. S. Lewis' Journey to Faith," https://www1.cbn.com/cs-lewis-journey-faith.

11. Harry Lee Poe, "10 Things You (Probably) Didn't Know about C. S. Lewis," *Publishers Weekly*, November 15, 2019, https://www.publishersweekly.com/pw/by-topic/industry-news/tip-sheet/article/81733-10-things-you-probably-didn-t-know-about-c-s-lewis.html.

12. David C. Downing, "C. S. Lewis as Atheist turned Apostle," published May 2, 2012, https://www.cslewis.com/c-s-lewis-as-atheist-turned-apostle/.
13. Melissa Cain Travis, *Science and the Mind of the Maker: What the Conversation between Faith and Science Reveals about God* (Eugene, OR: Harvest House Publishers, 2018), 22.
14. Nora Barlow, *The Autobiography of Charles Darwin* (London and Glasgow: Collins, 1958), 92–93, emphasis added.
15. Matthew Sleeth, *24/6: A Prescription for a Healthier, Happier Life* (Carol Stream, IL: Tyndale House, 2012), 105.
16. Linguistic, philosophical, and theological definitions of *naturalism* from Dictionary.com, https://www.dictionary.com/browse/naturalism, emphasis added.
17. Definition of *naturalist* from Dictionary.com, https://www.dictionary.com/browse/naturalist.
18. Definition of *naturalism* from Dictionary.com, https://www.dictionary.com/browse/naturalism.

### Chapter 3: Creation Groans . . . Until It Sings

1. InciWeb Incident Information System report of the Cameron Peak Fire, https://inciweb.nwcg.gov/incident/6964/.
2. Heather Hansen, *Wildfire: On the Front Lines with Station 8* (Seattle: Mountaineers Books, 2020), 170.
3. Rebecca Lindsey and Luann Dahlman, reviewed by Jessica Blunden, "Climate Change: Global Temperature," August 12, 2021, https://www.climate.gov/news-features/understanding-climate/climate-change-global-temperature.
4. Melissa Cain Travis, *Science and the Mind of the Maker: What the Conversation between Faith and Science Reveals about God* (Eugene, OR: Harvest House Publishers, 2018), 83.
5. Aldo Leopold, *A Sand County Almanac* (New York: Ballantine Books, 1966), 272–73.

6. John Muir, *Travels in Alaska* (Boston: Houghton Mifflin Company, 1915), 85.
7. See https://oceanservice.noaa.gov/news/jun22/seabed-2030.html.
8. William Rainey Harper, Ernest De Witt Burton, and Shailer Mathews, *The Biblical World*, vol. 30 (Chicago: University of Chicago Press, 1908), 70.

### Chapter 4: Nurturing Contagious Curiosity in Your Children
1. Earl Gustkey, "Black-Footed Animal, Once Believed Extinct, Has Surfaced in Wyoming; Curiosity-Seekers Head for Meeteetse: Mysterious Ferret Has 'Em Guessing," *Los Angeles Times*, March 17, 1985, https://www.latimes.com/archives/la-xpm-1985-03-17-sp-35545-story.html.
2. Oswald Chambers, *The Complete Works of Oswald Chambers* (Grand Rapids: Discovery House Publishers, 2013), 535.

### Chapter 5: Becoming a Wonder Conservationist
1. Aldo Leopold, *A Sand County Almanac* (New York: Ballantine Books, 1966), 246.
2. Kenn Kaufman, *A Season on the Wind: Inside the World of Spring Migration* (New York: Houghton Mifflin Harcourt, 2019), 5.
3. Johanna Spyri, *Heidi* (Philadelphia: J. B. Lippincott Company, 1915), 66.

### Chapter 6: The Absolute Truth About Nature
1. C. S Lewis, *Mere Christianity* (New York: HarperCollins, 2011), 38–39.
2. Hillary Morgan Ferrer, *Mama Bear Apologetics: Empowering Your Kids to Challenge Cultural Lies* (Eugene, OR: Harvest House Publishers, 2019), 143.
3. Lewis, *Mere Christianity*, 38.

4. Anna Botsford Comstock, *Handbook of Nature Study* (Ithaca: Comstock Publishing Company, 1922), 1.
5. Charlotte Mason, *The Outdoor Life of Children: The Importance of Nature Study and Outside Activities*, Charlotte Mason Topics (Independently published, 2015, from Charlotte Mason's works in the public domain), 4–5.
6. Melissa Cain Travis, *Science and the Mind of the Maker: What the Conversation between Faith and Science Reveals about God* (Eugene, OR: Harvest House Publishers, 2018), 79.
7. Travis, *Science and the Mind of the Maker*, 82.
8. Sally Clarkson, *Awaking Wonder: Opening Your Child's Heart to the Beauty of Learning* (Bloomington, MN: Bethany House, 2020), 14.
9. Cindy Ross, *The World Is Our Classroom: How One Family Used Nature and Travel to Shape an Extraordinary Education* (New York: Skyhorse Publishing, 2018), 11.
10. Ross, *World Is Our Classroom*, 23.
11. Oswald Chambers, *The Complete Works of Oswald Chambers* (Grand Rapids: Discovery House Publishers, 2013), 530.

### Chapter 7: Nature-Minded: Growing a Healthy Mindset Outdoors

1. See https://www.dictionary.com/browse/mindfulness.
2. Matthew Sleeth, *Reforesting Faith: What Trees Teach Us about the Nature of God and His Love for Us* (Colorado Springs: WaterBrook, 2019), 30–31.
3. John Muir, *The Yosemite* (New York: Century Co., 1912), 256.

### Chapter 8: Native Pastimes

1. Numbers comprised from Ginny Yurich, "Children Should be Outside for 4–6 Hours Every Day," *1000 Hours Outside* (blog), https://www.1000hoursoutside.com/blog/children-should-be

-outside-for-4-6-hours-everyday and Eryn Lynum, *936 Pennies: Discovering the Joy of Intentional Parenting* (Bloomington, MN: Bethany House, 2018), 214.

2. Douglas W. Tallamy, *Nature's Best Hope: A New Approach to Conservation That Starts in Your Yard* (Portland, OR: Timber Press, 2019), 94.

3. Eames Yates, "Here's why Steve Jobs never let his kids use an iPad," *Business Insider*, March 4, 2017, https://www.business insider.com/heres-why-steve-jobs-never-let-his-kids-use-ipad-apple-social-media-2017-3.

4. Gary Chapman and Arlene Pellicane, *Screen Kids: 5 Relational Skills Every Child Needs in a Tech-Driven World* (Chicago: Northfield Publishing, 2020), 13.

5. Eryn Lynum, *936 Pennies: Discovering the Joy of Intentional Parenting* (Bloomington, MN: Bethany House, 2018), 214.

6. Yurich, "Children Should be Outside for 4–6 Hours Every Day."

7. Louv, *Last Child in the Woods*, 36.

8. NASA Release 20-057, "NASA Astronauts Launch from America in Historic Test Flight of SpaceX Crew Dragon," May 30, 2020, https://www.nasa.gov/press-release/nasa-astro nauts-launch-from-america-in-historic-test-flight-of-spacex-crew-dragon.

9. Aldo Leopold, *A Sand County Almanac* (New York: Ballantine Books, 1966), 194.

10. Leopold, *Sand County Almanac*, 183.

11. Thank you to Curt Meine with the Aldo Leopold Foundation and Steve Brower with the Leopold Landscape Alliance in Burlington, IA, for researching and providing additional relevant information about Charles Wachsmuth, Frank Springer, and Margaret Morse Nice.

12. Leopold, *Sand County Almanac*, 205.

### Chapter 9: Nature's Time Capsule

1. As quoted by John Mark Comer, *The Ruthless Elimination of Hurry: How to Stay Emotionally Healthy and Spiritually Alive in the Chaos of the Modern World* (Colorado Springs: WaterBrook, 2019), 20.
2. Matthew Sleeth, *24/6: A Prescription for a Healthier, Happier Life* (Carol Stream, IL: Tyndale House, 2012), 91.
3. Sleeth, *24/6*, 93.

### Chapter 10: Family Hibernation

1. John Mark Comer, *The Ruthless Elimination of Hurry: How to Stay Emotionally Healthy and Spiritually Alive in the Chaos of the Modern World* (Colorado Springs: WaterBrook, 2019), 30.
2. Comer, *Ruthless Elimination of Hurry*, 31.

### Chapter 11: Creation and Creativity

1. Jolie Li, "Shinkansen: The bullet train inspired by Kingfishers," April 19, 2021, https://uxdesign.cc/shinkansen-the-bullet-train-inspired-by-kingfishers-bf6173cc5eae.
2. Melissa Cain Travis, *Science and the Mind of the Maker: What the Conversation between Faith and Science Reveals about God* (Eugene, OR: Harvest House Publishers, 2018), 137.
3. Austin Kleon, *Steal Like an Artist: 10 Things Nobody Told You About Being Creative* (New York: Workman Publishing, 2012), 36.
4. Travis, *Science and the Mind of the Maker*, 138–39.
5. John Muir, *A Thousand-Mile Walk to the Gulf* (Boston: Houghton Mifflin, 1916), xvi.
6. John Muir, *John Muir: His Life and Letters and Other Writings* (Hinckley, UK: Bâton Wicks, 1996), 186.
7. William Frederic Badè, *The Life and Letters of John Muir* (Boston: Houghton Mifflin, 1923), 155.

8. William Paley, *Natural Theology* (Oxford: Benediction Classics, 2017), 18.
9. Bruce Barton, *The Man Nobody Knows* (Indianapolis: Bobbs-Merrill Company, 1925), 30.
10. John Mark Comer, *The Ruthless Elimination of Hurry: How to Stay Emotionally Healthy and Spiritually Alive in the Chaos of the Modern World* (Colorado Springs: WaterBrook, 2019), 63.

## Chapter 12: Bringing Nature Indoors
1. Laura Ingalls, *Big Wisdom (Little Book): 1,001 Proverbs, Adages, and Precepts to Help You Live a Better Life* (Nashville: Thomas Nelson, 2005), 96.
2 Roger S. Ulrich, PhD, *Health Benefits of Gardens in Hospitals*, 2002, https://www.researchgate.net/publication/252307449 _Health_Benefits_of_Gardens_in_Hospitals.
3 Ulrich, *Health Benefits of Gardens in Hospitals*.
4. Jim Robbins, "Ecopsychology: How Immersion in Nature Benefits Your Health," January 9, 2020, https://e360.yale.edu /features/ecopsychology-how-immersion-in-nature-benefits -your-health.
5. Anne Frank, *The Diary of a Young Girl* (New York: Anchor Books, 1996), 136.
6. Michelle Krowl, "New Online: Theodore Roosevelt Papers," Library of Congress, October 17, 2018, https://blogs.loc.gov /loc/2018/10/new-online-theodore-roosevelt-papers/.
7. US Department of the Interior, "The Conservation Legacy of Theodore Roosevelt," February 14, 2020, https://www.doi .gov/blog/conservation-legacy-theodore-roosevelt.
8. J. Drew Lanham, *The Home Place: Memoirs of a Colored Man's Love Affair with Nature* (Minneapolis: Milkweed Editions, 2016), 31.

### Chapter 13: Unshakable Faith

1. William Paley, *Natural Theology* (Oxford: Benediction Classics, 2017), 31.
2. Melissa Cain Travis, *Science and the Mind of the Maker: What the Conversation between Faith and Science Reveals about God* (Eugene, OR: Harvest House Publishers, 2018), 90–91.
3. Travis, *Science and the Mind of the Maker*, 93–94.
4. Helen Macdonald, *Vesper Flights* (New York: Grove Atlantic, 2020), 94.
5. Aldo Leopold, *A Sand County Almanac* (New York: Ballantine Books, 1966), 230–32.

# About the Author

ERYN LYNUM IS A CERTIFIED master naturalist, Bible teacher, national speaker, and author of 936 *Pennies: Discovering the Joy of Intentional Parenting* and *Rooted in Wonder: Nurturing Your Family's Faith Through God's Creation*. Eryn lives in Northern Colorado with her husband, Grayson, and their four children, whom they homeschool—mainly in the great outdoors. Her family spends their days hiking, camping, and adventuring through the Rocky Mountains. Eryn leads nature classes and hikes and has been featured on *Focus on the Family, FamilyLife,* Proverbs 31 Ministries, *Christian Parenting, MOPS International, Bible Gateway, Her View From Home,* and *For Every Mom.* Every opportunity she gets, she is out exploring God's creation with her family and sharing the adventures at www.ErynLynum.com.